Real Time Ministry

Cycle B Sermons for Pentecost through
Proper 17 Based on the Gospel Texts

David Coffin

CSS Publishing Company, Inc.
Lima, Ohio

REAL TIME MINISTRY

FIRST EDITION
Copyright © 2020
by CSS Publishing Co., Inc.

Scripture quotations marked (RSV) are from the Revised Standard Version of the Bible, copyrighted 1946, 1952 ©, 1971, 1973, by the Division of Christian Education of the National Council of the Churches of Christ in the USA. Used by permission.

Library of Congress Cataloging-in-Publication Data:

Names: Coffin, David (Pastor), author. Title: Real time ministry : cycle B sermons for Pentecost through proper 17 based on the gospel texts / David Coffin. Identifiers: LCCN 2020026661 | ISBN 9780788029950 (paperback) | ISBN 9780788029967 (ebook) Subjects: LCSH: Bible. Mark--Sermons. | Bible. John--Sermons. | Common lectionary (1992). Year B. | Pentecost--Sermons. | Church year sermons. Classification: LCC BS2585.54 .C64 2020 | DDC 252/.64--dc23

For more information about CSS Publishing Company resources, visit our website at www. csspub.com, email us at csr@csspub.com, or call (800) 241-4056.

e-book:
ISBN-13: 978-0-7880-2996-7
ISBN-10: 0-7880-2996-7

ISBN-13: 978-0-7880-2995-0
ISBN-10: 0-7880-2995-9

DIGITALLY PRINTED

Contents

Introduction   *4*

Advocating For Whom?   *7*
Pentecost
John 5:26-27; 16:4b-15

Where's God?   *12*
Trinity Sunday
John 16:12-15

Family Ties And Unties   *17*
Proper 5 / Ordinary Time 10 / Pentecost 2
Mark: 3:20-35

Kingdom Mystery   *21*
Proper 6 / Ordinary Time 11 / Pentecost 3
Mark 4:24-36

Building Trust   *25*
Proper 7 / Ordinary Time 12 / Pentecost 4
Mark 4:35-41

New Life Goes On   *29*
Proper 8 / Ordinary Time 13 / Pentecost 5
Mark 5:21-43

Prophet Without Honor   *34*
Proper 9 / Ordinary Time 14 / Pentecost 6
Mark 3:6-13

Which Kingdom Do We Serve?   *38*
Proper 10 / Ordinary Time 15 / Pentecost 7
Mark 6:14-29

Gathered Around Jesus   *43*

Proper 11 / Ordinary Time 16 / Pentecost 8
Mark 6:30-34; 53-56

The Loaves   *48*

Proper 12 / Ordinary Time 17 / Pentecost 9
John 6:1-21

More Than Gimmicks   *53*

Proper 13 / Ordinary Time 18 / Pentecost 10
John 6:24-35

Bread And Call   *58*

Proper 14 / Ordinary Time 19 / Pentecost 11
John 6:35, 41-51

Belonging At The Table   *63*

Proper 15 / Ordinary Time 20 / Pentecost 12
John 6:51-58

Lord To Whom Shall We Go?   *67*

Proper 16 / Ordinary Time 21 / Pentcost 13
John 6:56-69

When The Rules Change   *72*

Proper 17 / Ordinary Time 22 / Pentecost 14
Mark 7:1-8, 14-15, 21-23

Introduction

To be a Christian today, in what many modern writers label a post-Christian North America, I believe we need to bring something to the table regarding matters of faith, religion and life application. This applies to both paid ministers as well as church laypersons that are active in their congregations. God's word contained in scripture has served this purpose for centuries alongside the sacraments or "rites" of baptism and communion (depending on your church fellowship). This collection of sermons is my effort to identify real problems and concerns which I have encountered in both my personal life and my thirty two years of pastoral ministry. The assumption of my sermons is that God's word in the Christian scriptures has some insights and good news for people whose lives have been disrupted, challenged in new ways as well as communities of faith who have lingering doubts regarding the future of the church. These sermons are based on real experiences I have had in ministry. The names and locations have been altered for privacy reasons.

This book is as much about my own experience in the church as well as the people involved. For better or for worse, I am a small town rural pastor in a financially struggling parish. I love this vocation very much despite the reality of many brutal setbacks I have experienced. However, I would like to thank those congregations, church leaders, judicatory staff, colleagues, and community members who have all helped shape my personal faith and ministry. I have included both positive and negative people who have influenced my life in this book of sermons. This book might be my "magnus opus" as a rural pastor serving in a fairly remote area of the American midwest. I make no apology for this. If I die today, I can go to my rest knowing that I have accomplished what God has placed me on the earth to do. I pray for this blessing for the readers of this. God places us where He needs us at any given time in history.

Also, I wish to thank Karyl Corson, David Runk, and the staff at CSS Publishing Company for their patience and hard work. Before being ordained as a Lutheran pastor, I worked in the printing industry in high school, college, and years after college. This field has also seen radical changes by technologies. I respect the people who work in this industry, as I recall the hectic time schedules, tight time lines, and relatively low profit margins of many printing companies whom I was employed. My pastoral colleagues, wife Barbara, and my sister Judy Milhim have been close confidants for me in my times of "writer's block" and doubt. Thank you to all.

David Coffin, Pastor
September 2019

Advocating For Whom?

In March of 2019, a New Hampshire lunch cafeteria worker was fired for giving a high school student an $8.00 meal because there was no money left in his account. She saw the student's lunch account was empty as he went through the line and allowed him to keep his food. She also asked him to have his mother add money to the account. The next day, the mother paid his lunch bill. However, the cafeteria manager who witnessed her act of leniency fired her. This quiet hero might be an advocate for students, as well as for Christ who fed five thousand people in John 6: 1-15.

In John 15 and 16, Jesus promised the Spirit will guide the disciples into all truth. In the world of John's gospel, "truth' is that which has proven to be reliable, reality, sure which possess the right motives. There is either light or darkness (John 1:1-14 RSV). The light who is Jesus or God in the flesh and the darkness does not overcome it. To believe in the name of the one who is light in the world is to become children of God. Thus, for Jesus in John's gospel, there is no gray area. One is either a child of the light or darkness. The lunch room lady illustration is a reminder that all people are often put on the spot to be an advocate for one position or another. Jesus was with the disciples at this point of the gospel narrative. However, he would go to his Father and the disciples would see him no longer (John 16:10 RSV). How does one "advocate for Jesus" — once he has departed?

According to our gospel lesson, the advocate would teach the world about sin, righteousness, and judgment (John 16: 9-11 RSV). Whenever I conduct funerals, quite often the question is asked why their loved one died. I respond it is because of "sin." The advocate reminds people of faith of their sin. In modern times this can prove to be difficult as to what is defined as "sin." Most Christians view the ten commandments in Exodus 20 as a point of reference as to what it means to disobey God and sin. For example, we may see a story on television about a person running in the park and being violently murdered. Our instant gut instincts tell us that this is wrong! Also, if we read about a store being broken into at night and merchandise stolen, we immediately identify this as wrong! It is the fifth and seventh commandments in Exodus 20 at stake here. Jesus in John's gospel calls us to a relationship with him and the community of faith. So let's take the third commandment for example here.

A church member decides to sleep in on Sunday morning, simply because they do not feel like attending worship that morning. Later, that late morning or early afternoon, they go to the local grocery store and lo and behold, there is the pastor from their church also picking up some items. If the person takes the third commandment seriously, "Remember the sabbath day to keep it holy," then the pastor's presence may elicit guilt. Had the same person gone to church, but happened to have either gone to Saturday evening worship or attended worship at another church, the presence of the pastor in the store is good news. People of faith do gather together to worship Christ and have fellowship with his people weekly. In John's writings, 1 John 1:7 (RSV), the author wrote, "but if we walk in the light, as he is in the light, we have fellowship with one another, and the blood of Jesus his Son cleanses us from all sin." The advocate reminds us that fellowship with God entails having fellowship with one another here in our church.

As this relates to the lunch lady in the opening illustration, it would be very comforting if she did have Bible study, or support group in her church to remind her that she was advocating for a child in need, just as the Spirit or advocate which Jesus Christ left would have her do. Furthermore, she is also serving others as a model of righteousness.

Jesus in John's gospel models righteousness in two ways. First, he washed his disciples' feet as an example of serving other people. Since many people walked on the dirt roads with either bare feet or sandals, foot washing was a major job. The water used probably got discolored rather rapidly. Righteousness was modeled here by washing the dirtier or messier parts of the person's body at that time. The lunch lady probably realized that it is very embarrassing for a high school student to hold up the cafeteria line with others behind him or her due to lack of funds. She served the student by allowing him to pass and would deal with the lack of money later. Was there anything in it for her? No, it was simply the right thing to do. This might be a modern example of foot washing.

Second, Jesus modeled righteousness by telling his disciples, "No longer do I call you servants, for the servant does not know what his Master is doing; but I have called you friends, for all that I have heard from my Father I have made known to you" (John 15:15 RSV). In the world of John, while Jesus is before the beginning with God, this same Messiah is unlike the top-down leaders of the Roman Empire who used power and coercion to accomplish their tasks. This Lord called his followers friends and left an advocate for us, rather than trying to micro-manage the creation with maybe the use of drones or high tech video technology. The advocate is an empowering force rather than coercive power.

Many communities of faith are actually good at this. When natural disasters occur such as floods, hurricanes, pandemics, or tornados, it is often faith-based communities who are present immediately after the disaster. Many of us in our congregation realize that we can be the next victim of any given disaster. We do support efforts to do clean up, set up temporary housing shelters, and provide medical or first aid attention. This is not a political position one takes. There is no democratic or republican position on dealing with an ice storm that takes out power lines or tornado levels whole communities. Meeting these folks in their time of turmoil is one example of foot washing as one of Jesus' disciples. Yet there are challenges which we still need help from an advocate when matters are not so cut and dry.

For example, a rural community decides they should set up a food pantry for needy families whose income is insufficient to meet the food needs of their family. There are cynics in every community who would say, "How do we know if we are not being taken advantage of by these folks? I might see them in the grocery store buying dog food after they are at the county food pantry." The civic groups and churches in charge decide that each family is to show identification that they are indeed residents of the county and that they have had their one visit to this food pantry. Is this too elitist or exclusive? What happens when a person who lives just over the county line comes in with crying children who need a meal? John's gospel would suggest the church err on the side of grace. But this might have consequences, such as, causing those who wish to cut the funding on such food programs to rise up. This is very similar to the lunch lady opening illustration. The advocate might prompt people to ask, "What would you want for your family or loved one who is in a similar situation?" In John's community, one honors Christ by treating other people in a humane manner — simply because it is the right thing to do.

John 3:16 (RSV) summarizes the gospel in a nutshell: "God loves the world so much that he gave his only Son, so all who believe in him will not perish." Jesus went on to say that he did not come to condemn the world, but that the world may be saved by him. The root Greek word for "saved" is "sodzo." This means to: deliver, keep safe, preserve, cure, or make well (Newman, 177). As for the food pantry illustration, on one hand it cannot be exploited or it will not be kept safe or preserved for anybody. On the other hand, one free extra gift should not break the food program either.

In this season of Pentecost or the mission of the church, we all need to be informed by the spirit or advocate based on our best senses of what it means to be a community of Christ. We are not to judge or condemn the world, but to cure its problems or make well in a time of darkness and sin. In John, one is either with the light or darkness (John 1:1-14 RSV).

Finally, the advocate's teaching of judgment is a sober reminder that sin, evil, and forces of darkness do exist. In the opening illustration, it was the inflexible rules of a corporate structure that would prefer the student without the lunch money go without, as well as penalize the lady who decided to be his advocate and allow the boy to pay back the eight dollars later. In the seasons of Pentecost, the church does confess in its creeds "he will come again to judge the living and the dead." What are we willing to die for, (or have our hour) so we may one day return and be among those stand before Christ's throne? For Jesus in John's gospel, his hour was that time he was raised up on the cross to die for the sins of humanity. He knew this way back in John 2 during the Cana wedding feast, when they ran out of wine and Jesus told his mother, "My hour has not yet come" (John 2:4 RSV). Throughout the gospel of John, Jesus had planned for his hour. This would result in him almost turning himself in to those who arrest him in John 18:5-6. Unlike the synoptic gospels, Jesus planned and prepared for his hour to come. He was then lifted up on the cross. Along with his time of death, it was and is also his time of glory.

Today, on Pentecost Sunday, we are invited to consider when our "hour" will come for us as a congregation. There has been much written on mainline churches in membership and financial decline. Rather than simply wait as victims, the good news of this text is that Jesus left us with an "advocate" to point us into the right direction. We are invited to ask for whom are we advocates? Where and when will the church in this season of Pentecost be willing to sacrifice or suffer the wrath of the world as disciples? It is an open-ended question for us to consider during this season.

Oh, by the way, I used to work at an office where if somebody was going out to a fast food lunch, they would ask if anyone else wanted them to pick up a sandwich, fries, or drink — and to please give them the right amount of money. How often does that work out?

Amen.

Sources:

Barclay Newman, *Greek English Dictionary of the New Testament* (New York: United Bible Societies, 1971).

Francis J. Maloney, Sacra Pagina: *The Gospel of John* (Collegeville, MN: The Liturgical Press, 1998).

D. Moody Smith, Abingdon *New Testament Commentaries: John,* (Nashville, TN: Abingdon Press, 1999).

Where's God?

Rather than taking a traditional, historical confessional approach to the doctrine of the Holy Trinity, I would like to suggest how this complex and mysterious teaching of the church might work in modern day situations. Imagine a person coming to worship on Holy Trinity Sunday who is not wondering if they will confess the lengthy Athanasian Creed. Rather, the person's mind is weighed down with the stunning news that their employer of 25 years is closing down the plant and company. All three hundred or so employees are told they have worked their last week there and a short amount of severance pay will be mailed to them in the coming weeks.

On Holy Trinity Sunday, where is God for those people who have lost their means of putting food on the table and keeping a roof over their head, as well as those who have lost their family health care benefits? Does their life have any meaning after the loss of a major source of income? Is there life after being disposed of like any commodity, which is of no longer any use to the modern high technology culture rendering people's entire lives as expendable for the sake of the financial bottom line? How does such a God of the Holy Trinity make any sense?

In John 3, we are introduced to a leader of the Jews, who is a learned Pharisee named Nicodemus. Many places in the New Testament give Pharisees a "bad name." However, secular historians of the time, such as Flavius Josephus, do not paint them in such a negative manner. Quite often they are asking legitimate questions that many people of faith are also asking. Nicodemus might be in this category. Not all of John's characters in his gospel are flat or single minded. Some are complex and are in a growing process. Joseph of Arimathea is another such person in John, as is the Samaritan woman at the well in John 4.

Nicodemus attempted to speak well of Jesus by acknowledging him as a teacher who performed signs from God. Much has been made about Nicodemus coming by night to suggest that he did not want to be seen in public with Jesus. Possibly he feared he would lose his position if he was spotted associating with Jesus. People who are terminated from a job quite often find that those whom they thought to be their friends are now cold, aloof, and keep their distance from the recently unemployed person. Jesus meets us where we are — even if it is a dark place at night. This is the nature of the Isaiah suffering servant story in Isaiah 52:12-53:13. This is God the Son or redeemer who is always with the creation of God. It is God the Son, or second person of the Trinity. God the Creator of the universe is one, yet in John's gospel, God comes in the flesh and dwells among God's creation (John 1:1-14 RSV).

Jesus responded with "Very truly I say to you…" In those days they did not have writing symbols for emphasis such as italics, underscoring or bold type. To emphasize a point had to be citied within the text itself. The Greek words *"Amayn, amayn"* (very truly) are an example of such a scribal tool to alert the readers or listener of the text. The main point is to enter the kingdom of God, one has to be born of water and spirit. Most Christian traditional beliefs are that baptism is necessary on the Christian journey. Some practice infant baptism for the entire family with biblical support from Matthew 28:16-20 (the great commission) and Acts 16 (the jailor and his whole family are baptized). Other faith traditions hold to a baptism event only after one has confessed Jesus as Savior and Lord. They can point to many conversion experiences in the Book of Acts to make this point. For the person whose job position is terminated, the point is that they are now part of the kingdom of God - not by their employment status but by virtue of their being born anew and baptized into the community of Christ. This is good news on Holy Trinity Sunday.

While John the Baptist's baptism was of water (John 1:26 RSV), the baptism into the kingdom of God which Jesus announces water and spirit. Jesus does not leave any people parentless or without guidance. He would remind the disciples of this before his arrest later in John 14:15-18, he leaves an advocate or counselor to all people of faith. Those who have recently lost their jobs are not alone. The God of creation who is the word made flesh (1:14 RSV) will leave his Spirit, and is mysteriously present with all people of faith.

The ancient church fathers wanted to affirm the tradition teaching of the one monotheistic God of Moses who gave us the Ten Commandments in Exodus 20. Yet, this God is doing a new act of creation by experiencing life's joys and sufferings beside us in the Son or suffering servant of Isaiah 52-53. This Son would redeem God's creation as we have in this text of John 3:16, which is often called the gospel in a nutshell, "For God so loved the world that he gave his only Son, that whoever believes in him should not perish but have eternal life" (John 3:16 RSV).

The promise to the person who is now unemployed is: God does not want any of God's creation to perish and does want them to have eternal life. Later in John 10:10, this God in the flesh named Jesus would say he wants us to have life and have it abundantly. This God promises both a length of life and quality of life. This is further good news for the people who have recently lost their jobs, loved ones or experience any other sort of recent tragedy. Where's God? God is mysteriously with each of us as God the Father (Creator), Son (redeemer) and Holy Spirit (sustainer). This may seem complex even to the learned of any age.

Nicodemus is no exception. One of John's literary tools is misunderstanding and irony. The Pharisee mistook being born again or from above as to return into one's mother's womb. The seconded "very truly" or *Amayn, Amayn*, is that the Jesus who teaches his disciples his ways will one day ascend back up the Father, or Creator. The Christian church is ultimately a community of faith. When the certitudes of science, credentialed education, and the benefits of the technology let us down, the church promises a Creator God who does not abandon God's creation but instead leaves us a spirit of life. This is one God and this God has three expressions.

Later in John's gospel, Nicodemus' faith evolved. He was a voice reminding his Sanhedrin colleagues that Jesus' words and ideas need to be carefully weighed according to the Hebrew Bible laws, rather than simple knee jerk opinions by angered leaders. After Jesus is crucified, he provides customary embalming spices for Jesus' body to assist Joseph of Arimathea in the burial of the body (John 19:39-42 RSV). Jesus has given this inquiring Pharisee Nicodemus a sense of meaning for his life, even though he might not have all the details down regarding born of the flesh, spirit, or eternal life.

The story is told that once the theologian Reinhold Niebuhr grew frustrated as he was doing congregational ministry in an industrialized Detroit, Michigan, neighborhood. The technology of the time was superior to that of past ages, in terms of the invention of automobiles, electricity, light bulbs, radio, and many forms of entertainment such as the phonograph, later to be called the record player. With all of these advances, Niebuhr saw Henry Ford the automaker exploiting his workers in dirty factories and for low wages. At first, Niebuhr was attracted to the Marxist system of government or community owned industries. He thought maybe the worker or the proletariat should be in charge of the economic means of producing wealth. Later, he saw the

Soviet Union's abuse and exploitation of its workers and farm laborers. Some even suggested that the Soviet leader Joseph Stalin murdered and abused far more of his citizens than Adolf Hitler had. Human sin remains the culprit! Finally, Niebuhr threw his hands up in the air and realized that higher education, technology, and material gain would not solve the spiritual problem of inner emptiness as a result of sin. It is all a matter of faith in a God who cannot be controlled or manipulated. As soon as we find such a God, humans try to control and manipulate this same God. A later theologian, Wolfhart Pannenberg, would make the same observation in one of his volumes that led to this three-volume systematic theology.

The apocryphal story continues about Reinhold Niebuhr whose disgust with both the capitalist and communist systems led him to write a prayer, "God grant me the serenity to accept the things I cannot change; courage to change the things I can; and wisdom to know the difference." This is now known as the Reinhold Niebuhr, *Serenity Prayer*, 1951. Later on two founders of the Alcoholics Anonymous movement Bill Wilson and Bob Smith would make much use of this prayer a major tool for recovery for those who sought to fill their holes in their souls with alcoholic beverages.

On this Holy Trinity Sunday, I would suggest that it is not as important to know about all of the historical debates, conflicts, and heretical concerns that led to this confession of God as Father, Son, and Holy Spirit. Rather it is more important how this cherished confession provides life to the church — especially for those who have lost that which is very valuable to them such as their means of employment. Any unemployed person, or a person who has recently experienced a tragic loss may rest their head on their pillows at night with the confidence that whoever believes in Jesus as the suffering servant, risen Lord and spiritual advocate indeed has eternal life. Where's God? God is present to all of us in the name of the Father, and of the Son, and of the Holy Spirit.

Amen.

Sources:

Alcoholics Anonymous (New York: Alcoholics Anonymous World Services, 1939).

Johannes Beutler, *S.J. A Commentary on the Gospel of John,* (Grand Rapids, MI: Wm. B. Erdmann's Publishing Co., 2017).

Niebuhr, Reinhold, *The Nature and Destiny of Man: A Christian Interpretation, 2 Volumes,* (Louisville, KY: Westminster John Knox Press, 1943).

Wolfhart Pannenberg, *An Introduction to Systematic Theology,* (Grand Rapids, MI: Wm. B. Erdmann's Publishing Co., 1991).

Family Ties And Unties

In the 1993 movie *Rudy*, Sean Astin plays Rudy Rudiger, a young man who grew up in a Roman Catholic working class family that was employed at the steel mills, which is major town economic bedrock. Rudy always wanted to play football for the University of Notre Dame. There were a couple problems. First, he was short, lacked strong talent, and he had difficulty in school due to dyslexia. His family and girlfriend all thought that he would fail in this venture. At age 22, when his best friend Pete died in an industrial accident, Rudy set out to pursue his dream. He discovered he was woefully unqualified to enroll in the University of Notre Dame. However, a local Catholic priest helped Rudy get into Holy Cross Junior College, where he met a tutor and worked as a groundskeeper. After many failed efforts to get into Notre Dame, he was finally accepted and was a walk-on player. He was part of the team as the tackling dummy and red shirt squad that performed the opposing teams' plays. He inspired the rest of the Notre Dame players to the point that they insisted that he gets to have field time for their final season game against Georgia Tech. The young man who everybody thought to be unrealistic and at times out of his mind, was finally carried off the field in victory by his fellow teammates.

In Mark 3, Jesus' family thought he "had gone out of his mind." They sought to restrain him. The reader of Mark, knew that Jesus was God's "beloved Son, whom he is well pleased," as he was baptized by John. Jesus had survived forty days in the wilderness, being tempted by Satan (Mark 1:12-13 RSV). He had performed healings and called his disciples (including Judas). If one assumed Jesus' father was a craftsman or carpenter of sorts, Jesus was going off the family reservation of the family vocational calling, as Rudy did in abandoning his job at the steel mills to pursue an education at the University of Notre Dame.

In the midwest states of America, there once were many factory towns which served as an economic base, and major sources of employment and medical benefits for many families. This went on for generations since the industrial revolution came to America. Some people were happy to have the job and income, while others complained about the dirty factory conditions, loud noises that impaired hearing, and the sporadic layoffs due to labor union disputes or changeover of model cars for the next year. Some families desired to pass the factory work tradition onto the next generations — and even viewed such well-paying jobs as entitlements of sorts. Other people did go into higher education in hopes of escaping the dirty shop conditions and seeking better working conditions, with more vocational mobility. To do the latter meant risks. Jesus took a similar risk in leaving the family trade tradition. He would be untied from the family.

One of the features of Mark's gospel is that the gospel writer "sandwiches" or intercalates a "story within a story." This text is an example. The scribes came down from Jerusalem to inquire, if not to interrogate Jesus as to where he gets his power to heal and forgive sins. In today's terms, they might be the accrediting agency's inspection team that makes periodic visits to community schools and colleges to make sure the school is maintaining high enough standards to be listed as "accredited."

John Grisham has written a book titled, *The Rooster Bar*. Roughly, the plot is based around law school students who discover in their final year that their school is barely accredited; their degrees are worthless; and they are now way over their heads in higher education debt. One can watch the news and realize that the problem of high student debt rings true for many families as they plan to send their family members to college. The scribes are visiting Jesus to see if his works are "accredited" from God as they understand God, or is Jesus in league with Beelzebub (Satan)?

Not recognizing the source of Jesus' power, they framed their questions around the assumption that if one is able to cast out Satan's demons, this person must be an ally or in league with Satan. This is also called "demonizing" the other person.

To use another sports illustration, some levels of sports competition in all athletics may often be tempted to describe the opposing team members as less than human, the enemy as obstacles to their future of having a successful athletic career. It is easy to "dehumanize" people we do not happen to like so as to aggressively attack them not only to win, but to annihilate them. We will see some athletes who run up the scores as they win and take "victory dances" not only to win, but to shame the opposing team. It is like rubbing their face in the defeat. This does not have to be the case. One can oppose somebody's ideas without striving to "demonize" them, as the scribes are attempting to do with Jesus here in Mark 3.

More positive examples of athletic competition include when a particular team is hurt or has lost loved ones. The 1970 movie *We Are Marshall* was about Marshall University's football team and coaches getting killed in an air disaster, and the new coach who tried to rebuild the football team in West Virginia. After efforts to hire a coach and organize a new football team, the rival football team coach in West Virginia allowed the newly formed Marshall coaching staff to view their game films. Also, opposing teams wore an "M" on the back of their football helmets as a way to remember and honor the deceased Marshall football team.

In our Mark 3 text, Jesus reframed the assumption of the scribes and suggested that a house divided cannot stand. If Satan had used Jesus to cast out his own demons, then Satan's domain would not last long. One cannot plunder an owner's house without first restraining the owner.

Jesus also produced a verbal counter punch to suggest that he was indeed sent from God to forgive sins. Those who reject him, also reject the Spirit and Father God who sent him. This is defined as blasphemy, or the unpardonable sin: that is to reject God's Spirit in Jesus the Christ.

Historically, many writers and theologians have written about what exactly the unpardonable sin is. Is it lack of repentance? Possibly it is resisting God's grace or acting like a "reprobate," as the old Calvinists suggested. This particular passage suggests it is simply rejecting Jesus' power to forgive, heal, and his saving act of death on the cross. For Mark, Jesus became the "Messiah" as he died on the cross for the sins of humanity. Mark 10:45 (RSV) is a summary of Jesus' mission in Mark, "For the Son of Man also came not to be served but to serve, and to give his life as a ransom for many." The Scribes insisted that Jesus had an "unclean spirit." He did not convince them otherwise, despite his best efforts of persuasion.

This is a reminder to Christians everywhere that we can make our best case both in actions and verbs, and certain people and groups will still remain unconvinced and will still oppose our efforts as disciples. This is not a modern evangelistic crusade where auditoriums of people gather in for praise music, to listen to testimonies and a sermon, then are invited to an altar call. Mark's gospel keeps it real! Powerful people crave more power and are not going to compromise, despite the best argued logic, good intentions, and selfless acts of sacrifice. Martin Luther would argue we are saint and sinner at the same time.

The story in Mark 3 continues with Jesus' identifying his true family. They are also a part of the kingdom of God. In our modern times, quite often people of faith are at odds with one another based on their particular view of sacred scriptures and how they apply to daily life. Our lives are already framed with a background or worldview that has shaped us. In the 1980s and 1990s, there were many popular movies about how getting into college and obtaining the goal as the leading fraternity, sorority or *Revenge of the Nerds*, was seen as an end in and of itself. In our modern days, there is the sticker shock heavy student loan debt and fear of jobs that may become automated. The old family work tradition can either be mechanized or is diminishing significance with major wholesale outlets and online purchasing services.

In some rural communities, there are legitimate fears as to how long certain family farms can keep going. Between unpredictable weather conditions and fluctuating prices for both various forms of livestock and grains, farmers often live by as much urgent faith as those ancestors did in the Hebrew Bible or Old Testament. The God who sustained Abraham's offspring throughout scripture, will also sustain us in our communities today. God is full of second chances regardless of any errors made on our end. This part of the good news found in Mark's gospel.

Jesus in Mark's gospel still has a place for all people who either stayed with the family ties or are have been untied to the family traditions. That is, all who do follow Jesus' teachings and will as disciples are already part of the kingdom of God. Jesus looked at the crowds all around him, many who are nameless peasants, and people who will never have a book written or movie made about them. He tells them, "Whoever does the will of God is my brother, and sister, and mother." This is the good news of the gospel lesson today. Regardless of whether our churches are struggling, have a spot on the local radio and newspaper, or if they are live streamed — whoever does the will of God are Jesus' brothers and sisters.

Amen.

Sources:

Daniel J. Harrington S.J., Sacra Pagina: *The Gospel of Mark*, (Collegeville, MN: The Liturgical Press, 2002).

John Grisham, *The Rooster Bar*, (New York: Doubleday Press, 2018).

Proper 6 / Ordinary Time 11 / Pentecost 3

Mark 4:24-36

Kingdom Mystery

An older man in his early sixties of age has been working for his company for over 25 years. He attended college and later went back for a master's degree so he could better serve his employer. He has earned his own office due to his hard work. While he is not a regular church worshiper, he does practice the Christian work ethic he learned earlier in life regarding working hard today for a better future. He is honest and will help people who in are need. He tries to model this work ethic for his family and friends. As his hard work and efforts seems to be paying off in successful and stable life, change, and tragedy suddenly occurs!

His employer sold the company to an international conglomerate who shifted all employee positions from offices to small cubicles with no privacy. His age makes him a very difficult candidate for the area employment market, which is seeking younger workers — recent graduates from college with high energy levels and new ideas. His wife of many years died as a result of a car accident on the horrific storms of wintry icy roads in his state. He was raising his granddaughter because his adult daughter was perpetually in and out of both personal relationships and employers. As he talked to his Christian friend, he pleaded, "If God's kingdom is coming and is so mysterious, please don't send me to hell if I don't guess right." How do the seeds of the kingdom of God provide comfort and good news to people whom we know who simply always have bad luck, despite their own honest hard work and sincere efforts to get ahead in life?

Mark 4 is one of the longer set of teachings which Jesus provided in the gospel, beside the Mark 13 apocalyptic discourse. The theme is how the kingdom of God arrived and works to transform the world even now. The assumption is that this is God's world, which God created and continues to create. Mark is the first synoptic gospel to be written, usually dated around 65-70 CE. Later gospel writers Matthew and Luke used portions of Mark's gospel along with a separate unidentified source known as "Q." Mark wrote to a persecuted community of faith who were under the heavy handed violent yoke of the ruling empire of Rome.

The Jerusalem temple had been or would soon be destroyed by Roman troops in the midst of a Judean revolt against the imperial hardships of living under the Roman yoke.

After baptism, wilderness temptation, and a series of healings, Jesus shared parables related to seeds as they relate to the kingdom of God. This text follows the parable of the sower who sows seeds which falls on varying types of soil with mixed results. Jesus' point in today's text is God's kingdom is still arriving even though we wonder how and when.

"He also said, "The kingdom of God is as if someone would scatter seed on the ground, and would sleep and rise night and day, and the seed would sprout and grow, he does not know how" Mark 4:26-27 (RSV). If the reader is discouraged by the previous parable that has only one of four groups of planted seeds producing fruit, this text is good news. The sower in this parable is fairly random in planting of seeds. The sower does get time to sleep and rest. Then in some mysterious way, the seeds sprout and grow. The sower does not know how.

The good news for churches and communities of faith such as ours is that somehow and in some way, God's kingdom is growing in our midst, regardless of our efforts. God's kingdom continues to take shape. Later in the text, the kingdom of God is similar to a mustard seed, "It is like a grain of mustard seed, which, when sown upon the ground, is the smallest of all the seeds on earth; yet when it is sown it grows up and becomes the greatest of all shrubs, and puts forth large branches, so that the birds of the air can make nests in its shade" Mark 4:31-32 (RSV). The good news of the kingdom of God arrives in a mysterious way despite our efforts. This is both God's grace and the nature of how seeds die and new life grows in their place.

Historically, I would commend to you the book titled, *"The Patient Ferment of the Early Church: The Improbable Rise of Christianity in the Roman Empire,"* by Alan Kreider. Before the conversion of Roman Emperor Constantine in the fourth Century CE, the Christian church was an outlawed, persecuted religion that had to compete with a number of other Greco-Roman belief systems. Like today, Christianity was simply one among many belief systems which were also quite tolerant. Their worshipers enjoyed many imperial benefits. Yet, Christianity grew by 40% per decade (Alan Kreider, *The Patient Ferment of the Early Church: The Improbable Rise of Christianity in the Roman Empire* (Grand Rapids, MI: Baker Academic, 2016), 8). Patience and practicing one's faith were the secrets to this slow fermenting growth, rather than missionary programs and outreach efforts.

To worship him is to glorify God and practice one's faith as learned in church catechumate, what we might call Christian education today. Christianity is a way of life, not a result of philosophical debates on the public square. Early church fathers such as Justin, Clement, Origen, Tertullian, and Cyprian taught patience, endurance, avoiding vengeance and walking in the footsteps of Jesus as taught in the wisdom and writings of their time. What we call the Old Testament, or Hebrew scriptures were well on the way to being established teachings then. This would include the wisdom books of Psalms and Proverbs. If one really believed that Jesus' death and resurrection has conquered the grave, there is little to fear from the Roman Empire patience, following Jesus' teachings and footsteps is both life giving, empowering and the best defense against any type of persecution (Alan Kreider, *The Patient Ferment*, 13-35).

The early church grew like fermentation similar to a substance that slowly breaks down and emerges into alcohol as organic and chemical changes occur in the organism. Besides alcoholic beverages, pickled cucumbers ferment into another color and taste of food. It takes time and patience. New life will come. This is what the early church realized even before the church became the state religion under Roman Emperor Constantine. It was the habits and discipleship lifestyle which attracted new converts to the church. These were times when people were disposable according to how young and attractive or productive in the imperial economy with its Greco-Roman religious leaders who endorsed values which make humans disposable commodities based on their economic and labor viability. It would be similar to an aging television newscaster being released from their work contract to be replaced by younger looking reporters. It was a religion of worshiping youth and beauty. Such people were welcomed in the church with their lifetime of wisdom and experience in the world.

Mark's audience needed to hear that God's kingdom would come and is in our midst — with or without aggressive human efforts. This is the good news of the text today. The kingdom is a mystery. As many traditional church congregations today wonder about their future, the good news of Mark 4 is God's kingdom will arrive. Just as sure as mustard seeds grown to become great bushes, and other seeds are planted and grow while the sower is asleep, the mystery of the kingdom is present here today in our community.

In response the man in the opening illustration, as he takes his granddaughter to summer church camp, has her do house chores and does other actions which model his work ethic (despite his employer's treatment at work), he is indeed planting seeds with his granddaughter. Also as her friends who visit them see and experience his sincere nurture, care and work ethic. God knows what is truly in his heart. Our task as Christians is to be in conversation with such people and model our discipleship as we have been taught in church for others to see and experience. It takes time to "ferment," but the mystery of the kingdom of God is that it is slowly arriving within this season of the church, called Pentecost.

Amen.

Sources:

John R. Donahue, S.J. and Daniel J. Harrington, S.J., *Sacra Pagina: The Gospel of Mark,* (Collegeville, MN: The Liturgical Press, 2002).

Alan Kreider, *The Patient Ferment of the Early Church: The Improbable Rise of Christianity in the Roman Empire,* (Grand Rapids, MI: Baker Academic, 2016).

Francis J. Maloney, *The Gospel of Mark: A Commentary,* (Peabody, MA: Hendrickson Publishers, 2002).

Building Trust

Imagine a family member receiving a late night phone call, in which the caller ID reads, "County Corrections." A close loved one is being held in custody due to an arrest of being intoxicated either on an alcoholic or opioid drug influence while driving their motor vehicle. The loved one needs the family member to immediately call them a lawyer and drive down to the county corrections facility. This is like being unexpectedly ambushed at night from a person whom we least expect to be acting like this. This continues as a long, nightmarish storm of chaos of living with a relative who is addicted to alcohol or some form of substance abuse.

As the story unfolds, the family member discovers that the loved one has run up credit cards to the point that collection agencies are pursuing them. There is the discovery that the loved uses their charm and family connections to get access to money for their substance of choice. The addict family member has repeatedly concocted lies and more lies to cover their footprint of dishonesty.

The next chapter of this gut wrenching storm includes court dates, court fees, lawyer's fees, and fees for random drug tests, ankle bracelet monitoring devices, and driving the person to their twelve-step group and counseling sessions. The loved ones automobile drivers' license has been suspended, so guess who is their new chauffeur? Also, there are the numerous amounts of statewide phone calls to treatment centers that may or may not be covered by the family insurance plan, and the time period as to when the loved one can be admitted into their program. This can take a couple days after one negotiates tedious phone banks, answering machines, and being put "on hold" for up to an hour's waiting time. Loving an addict is a very tumultuous time of nightmarish disruptions similar to the seas metaphor for similar chaos in the psalms and other parts of scripture.

After six months to a year of listening to, "I'm sorry," being late for commitments, and ignoring the alarm clock, those words are like annoying dead insects on the car windshield. How can trust ever be rebuilt again? There are only a small group of people the family member dares confide in as to how deeply and painfully this addiction battle has unraveled the family routines and schedules. In fact, this family member has to go to their doctor to get medication so they do not grind their teeth at night in anger, as they take natural herbs to fall asleep at night.

Where is Jesus here? Is Jesus sleeping on a cushion in the stern of the boat? Mark's gospel is an ongoing time of instruction for discipleship. Jesus is trying to build trust with his disciples. There are many test practices of how much faith the disciples have in Jesus. This Mark 4 text is one of such tests. Among the previous lessons taught include: teaching about Satan and family in Mark 3; the parable of the sower and mustard seed earlier in Mark 4.

Mark's gospel is written to small town and rural audience round 70 CE. He uses very basic *koine* Greek (instead of the highly educated classical Greek). Mark is not as polished in his writing skills as evangelist Luke, in his books of Luke and Acts. Thus, to learn in these small town rural communities means to practice what they are taught in terms of hands on application. For example, if a person wishes to earn a Veterinary Technician's Certificate, he or she must do more than read books and hear a lecture. They will have to physically place a suppository up an animal's rectum to relieve constipation related issues. They may have use dental floss to clean a dog's teeth to avoid tooth decay and extractions. Yes, the student might have quite a mess to clean up after the constipation issue is overcome as well as being bitten by the dog that is tasting dental floss. There are no short cuts to "discipleship" in this area of learning. Jesus also realized this.

Jesus was sleeping on the cushion on a boat while there was a great windstorm. How will the disciples apply what they have just learned thus far from Jesus? Many commentators consulted believe the disciples also had teachings from Psalm 107: 23-32. In this psalm, God has proven he is Lord over the waters of chaos while the people of faith are in distress. They rejoiced that God is Lord of all troubled waters which come into our lives. Can Jesus be trusted as "Lord" in the same way?

Another well-known biblical teaching was that of Jonah 1, as the prophet was on a ship to flee Nineveh on his way to Tarshish. A great storm arose as Jonah was asleep. While the water waves were splashing onto the ship's decks, Jonah was awakened by the ship's captain. After Jonah asked to be thrown overboard, the Lord calmed the sea afterward. Again, the Lord can be trusted. Simply reading and hearing of such events is not enough to grow as a disciple in Mark's gospel. The disciples must experience the Lord's finding them in their respective times of chaos and upheavals in life and trust to be delivered.

In the opening illustration, many families of alcoholics and addicts will accompany their loved one to treatment centers and 12-step meetings. The first immediate reaction is to purchase as many books and pamphlets on addiction and recovery as possible to read and digest the materials written on the pages of the printed materials. There is indeed an entire publishing industry who has dedicated itself of multiple printed editions of various recovery materials. Reading and listening is no replacement for human interaction by attending either a 12-step recovery group, faith-based support group or simply having a handful of trusted friends who are good at respecting confidentiality.

In such "hands on" experiences, the family member will discover that they no longer have to be terrorized by the addiction. They did not cause it, can't cure it, nor control it. But they can do something about their response to addictive behaviors. For example, creating healthy boundaries on ATM, checking, and other bank accounts is one practical way to practice recovery. Also, the family member needs a sponsor or close friend to "vent" with who will not judge them for rambling on about the same topic again and again. They must trust their sponsor or friend to call them out, when they observe unreasonable or unhealthy words and actions. The family member must accept the reality that their addicted loved one may relapse. Finally, the family member has to find a way to get on with his or her own life and that of the family's without allowing the addicted person's recovery or lack of recovery disrupt their lives, so they may have a measure of serenity. The family can avoid or limit exposure to alcohol or other substance parties and events. However, it will take time for them to build trust in the addict as the addict may or may not back track on their recovery journey. This is an ongoing lifestyle of living with an addicted person, which takes time and practice. This is precisely what Jesus is attempting to teach his disciples, as they will inevitably face persecution for their faith in the crucified and risen Jesus as Lord.

Historically, these disciples were not quick learners. By today's standards they flunked the ACT and SAT many times. They will have to attend community or junior college before they are ready to step up to the next level. The good news is Jesus does not give up on the disciples despite their failures. Jesus does not *give up on us* despite our own failures — be they on purpose or by mistake.

In Mark's gospel, the inner circle of chosen disciples actually grew worse and worse in their understanding of who Jesus was as Lord. It is often the outsiders such as the man who had the legion of demons cast into pigs in Mark 3 who really knew the identity of Jesus as Lord. The foreign Syrophoenician woman whose daughter had an unclean spirit recognized who Jesus truly was in Mark 7. Other good news of this text is if anybody has not made the "first cut" onto the team, this does not mean they are out of the game. They still know the plays, players, and rules of the game.

A modern example might be a young person who does not make it into their high school band due to very stiff competition. They and their friends form a garage band which results in many paid performances throughout the community in terms of county fair events, parties, and they were able to cut their own "CD" with a local recording company. Outsiders still have a chance in Mark's gospel — as the original inner circle will need more learning moments.

How many more teachable moments and practice lessons will the disciples in Mark need? This is an open-ended question. The other good news based on Mark 16:8, is the uncertainty of how the disciples responded to the empty tomb. Another recurring piece of good news in Mark's gospel is we all get to write the ending of our own story in life. The disciples will have another time at the plate in the batter's box. They will have another opportunity to run another sprint race or put on the shoulder pads for a football game in bad weather. God never gives up on God's people. Just as God did not give up on the stubborn Jonah in his refusal to preach to Nineveh, God does not give up on us or our loved ones, despite our refusal to listen to God. This is all part of the long process of building trust in this season of the church called Pentecost. I would bet you know of some people in our own pews who pride themselves as being "stubborn and thick headed!" It will take time to build trust. Jesus will not give up on these disciples. Jesus does not give up on us.

Amen.

Sources:

Al-Anon Family Group, *Paths to Recovery: Al-Anon's Steps, Traditions and Concepts,* (Virginia Beach, VA: Al-Anon Family Group Headquarters Inc, 1992).

Collins, *Adela Yarbro, Hermeneia: Mark,* (Minneapolis, MN: Fortress Press, 2007).

Donald A. Juel, *International Biblical Texts: The Gospel of Mark,* (Nashville, TN: Abingdon Press, 1999).

New Life Goes On

The experience is worse than any walk of shame one sees for people being voted off the program in any television reality show. A woman who is in her upper middle ages had been working in her mid-level management office job for twelve years. She had done all of the right things. She had both a bachelor's and master's degree in her field. Her colleagues enjoyed her, as did the people who worked in her department whom she supervised. She kept a cordial relationship with upper management. She wore company clothing with the corporate logo on her polo shirt. Her life was fully on schedule as two of her children were currently in college. What could go wrong?

One sunny Friday afternoon at 4:30 p.m. two armed uniformed security guards from the company headquarters entered her office. They presented her with a pink slip indicating that her position had been immediately terminated. They had an empty brown box in which she was ordered to place all of the personal belongings in her desk. One guard made sure nothing was taken that was company property (like a stapler or three-hole paper punch). As she was emptying the contents of her desk, the other security guard asked for her company ID badge. He logged onto her computer and deleted all files as he put in new passwords and username codes. The woman was still stunned! She was being "ambushed!" Could things get any worse? Yes, they could!

The two security guards ushered her down the aisles of workers whom she supervised and the colleagues whom she had known for twelve years both on the job and socially in family events. She carried the brown box out toward the parking lot, past the employee cafeteria with the guards closely following her. As she fought back tears, she was taking a final walk of shame to make a corporate power point to the other employees who had not been terminated yet. The office was so quiet one could hear a pin drop on the carpet floor. As she turned on the ignition of her car, she was directed to the parking lot exit. Upon leaving the premises, the parking lot gates were immediately closed and electronically locked. Was this the end of this humiliation? No!

That evening at the local restaurant where everybody hung out after work, the people whom all witnessed her embarrassing exit from the company premises, were as polite as they needed to be to her. But nobody wanted to be seen on camera sitting next to her or socializing with her. Being fired from the job carries a twofold of unwritten assumptions. First, that she did something wrong and the company had good reason to terminate her. Second, if anybody else is seen associating with her, they too could see their job on the "chopping block." This woman who was terminated after twelve years of faithful service could well empathize with the woman who had the blood hemorrhages, and was also a social outcast.

In Mark's gospel, it is the marginalized and unnamed outsiders who really understand who Jesus really is as the "Son of God" Mark 15:39 (RSV), The Centurion. The gospel lesson begins with illness of a twelve-year-old girl, who was the daughter of a synagogue leader named Jairus. This is one of the few times in Mark's gospel where a powerful person in the religious establishment had faith in Jesus' power to heal. This was good news for those who do hold varying positions of status and power in the community, from middle to upper class occupation. Jairus was still an "outsider" by Mark's standards. He was not one of Jesus' discipleship who had heard his teachings, witnessed his miracles, and was present at the casting out of demons. Jairus was certainly not one of the inner circles of disciples such as Peter, James, and John. Yet, he still had faith in Jesus' power. We never hear of him again in this gospel, although Matthew 9 and Luke 8 mention him.

Before Jesus arrived at Jairus' house, a named woman in the crowds who were following Jesus, touched Jesus' cloak. Scholars have written about this phenomenon for ages. There are those who identify other great Greek teachers and healers of the time who could heal people. There is the thought that a person's clothes as an extension of who they are as people. It would be like my wearing a t-shirt from my home high school as an alumnus, and somebody grabbing onto it. They have made physical contact of where I came from and who I am as the alumni of a given high school. Touching a person's garments could be viewed as a way of healing. In a modern politically correct atmosphere, the woman might be asked to attend a "boundaries workshop." The touch to Jesus is still worth the risk even for ten boundaries workshops!

The text reports that the other healing professionals of this woman's day were unsuccessful in healing her from the bleeding ailment. One commentator I read indicated that the physicians of her day had exhausted all of her financial resources and she was still not well. Her medical benefits had been exhausted for those twelve years. She probably got medical bills for the unpaid co-payments she owed to the medical establishment. She was still ill, and if she read Deuteronomy 15:1-6, she could file for bankruptcy once every seven years. Nobody wanted to be seen around a person like this. They are viewed as a loser, leech, and lackey of the society. She could identify with the woman in the opening illustration who was ambushed on late Friday afternoon by her employer.

She did touch Jesus' robe. The text says she was healed "immediately." Mark's gospel used this Greek word of *euthos* 42 times. Mark was writing to a small town, rural, working population. They did not have time on their side in terms of daily chores and errands. People in Mark's community must work quickly to get their chores done before nightfall. There is no time for chit chat or visiting. There is no time for a long Sermon on the Mount like in Matthew 5. There is no time for a "bread of life" discourse like in John 6. The woman was healed immediately. Jesus acknowledged, "Daughter, your faith has made you well; go in peace and be healed of your disease" Mark 5:34 (RSV).

Two observations here: Jesus addressed her as "daughter." She was not his child out of another relationship. Rather, we see a glimpse what Mark 1:1 meant when the gospel writer said, "The beginning of the gospel of Jesus Christ, the Son of God" Mark 1:1 (RSV). This Son of God was a healer so others may have new life. Her social outcast stigma was immediately removed. She could get on with her life. No, she was not present to see Jesus calm the stormy sea, or cast out demons. Nor did she hear any sermons Jesus gave to the disciples. She was an outsider who had simple faith in Jesus as Son of God. Life went on for her after twelve trying years. What a sigh of relief! Jesus wished her "peace." The Greek word *earaynee,* indicated her life was in harmony, and was in good order.

Mark liked to place a story within a story as a literary tool to make theological points. The narrative of Jairus' daughter continued as the synagogue leader received news that his daughter was dead. The mourners in the community were already in the house weeping and wailing. Jesus indicated that the child was not dead, but asleep. Jesus used the Aramaic words for "daughter get up!" She immediately (use of that *euthos* word again) got up and walked. All were overcome with amazement.

New life for this girl was similar to that of Lazarus in John 11. In John's gospel for Jesus to have such a power over life and death was viewed as a threat to the Judean authorities. In Mark, people were amazed. The girl was given a meal to eat and Jesus ordered strict secrecy of this miracle. We already see a glimpse of resurrection teachings here in Mark's gospel. Scholars have often pointed to the abrupt ending in Mark 16:8, where the women are simply frightened but nobody has yet seen the risen Christ. This text and the passion prediction in Mark 9:31 (RSV) ("The Son of man will be delivered into the hands of men, and they will kill him; and when he is killed, after three days he will rise") are signs that the gospel writer did intend to show the reader that Jesus' resurrection from the grave was real. Those, whose faith is in this Jesus, will also have a new life like his. This is more good news of the text.

Why the secrecy? This is called the "messianic secret" that is unique to Mark's gospel. There have been volumes written on this and we will not resolve the scholarly issues this day. I happen to believe that Jesus did not want people to identify him as Messiah or Son of God until he died on the cross for the sins of humanity and rose from the grave three days later. In Mark, Jesus became the Messianic Son of God when he died on the cross. He was not to be mistaken as an itinerant healing, feeding exorcist service. To be part of the kingdom of God in Mark was to simply have faith in Jesus and trust God for new life.

Where is the kingdom of God in Mark's gospel? It can be among the religious establishment people of the time such as Jairus, his household, and the community who supported him. The kingdom was also among the outsiders such as the nameless woman who was healed simply, for having faith in Jesus' power from God. Jairus' daughter could grow up, get married, and have a family of her own. Nobody told them they had to quit the synagogue. New life goes on!

The woman in the opening story found a small community of faith who connected her with a self-employment opportunity in which she still flourishes to this very day. She found new life. Again, new life went on for her as well. The good news of Jesus' healings today is that that the kingdom was simply not being released from the hospital or physicians care then going home to live like a coach potato for a month or so. The kingdom of God is where people are healed and find new life as a witness to whom this crucified and risen Messiah is in our lives. This is also the spirit of the Pentecost season when the church does its ministry. An example might be that a pastor visited a homebound church member who was recuperating from surgery in a nursing home. The person did not want to lie on the bed all day. They got a box of greeting cards and wrote them to people in their family and community. This is indeed ministry! I don't know about you, but isn't it great when we can get something besides "junk and bills" in the mail?

Amen.

Sources:

Adela Yarbro Collins, *Hermeneia: Mark: A Commentary on the Gospel of Mark,* (Minneapolis, MN: Fortress Press, 2007).

Morna Hooker, *Black's New Testament Commentaries: The Gospel of St. Mark,* (Peabody, MA: Hendrickson Publishers, 1991).

Juel, Donald, *Interpreting Biblical Texts: The Gospel of Mark,* (Nashville, TN: Abingdon Press, 1999).

Barclay Newman, *Greek-English Dictionary of the New Testament* (New York: United Bible Societies, 1971).

Prophet Without Honor

Imagine a high school student who was struggling with his math homework. His father was in a high-tech machine occupation in which he worked with much complicated math. He sat down at the table to help the student with the math homework. Unfortunately, the father was not a good instructor because he lacked patience in trying to help the student out who was not too savvy with numbers and figures. The child could not relate to his father as an instructor or teacher. He was the dad who worked around the house with outdoor chores, went to work to earn a living, and liked to take the family to area sports events. He was not a teacher by any stretch of the imagination. The student was frustrated and told the father he would seek help elsewhere with a tutor or another student whom he knew to be skilled at high school mathematics. The father was otherwise very good with the use of math where he worked. However, at home, his mathematics abilities made him a prophet without honor.

In the same community, a young man had been working for an area manufacturer, and one day decided he did not want to work in this factory or its office anymore. He felt called to become an ordained Christian pastor. He went through all of the denomination's requirements, attended their seminary and then decided he wished to return home to interview for a pastoral vacancy in the area. The interview went well, but the congregation decided to call a retired armed forces chaplain instead. They told the young man that while they knew him and his family background, they could not see him as their "pastor-*per se*," he would always be associated as an employee at the major manufacturer in town. Welcome to the world of Jesus in our Mark 6 lesson today.

The story of Jesus being rejected in his home town of Nazareth is also cited in Matthew 13 and Luke 4. This means it was well known by all of the synoptic gospel writers. In Luke's gospel, the home town crowd expects some special consideration in terms of more ministry, miracles and feeding since he was the son of the community. In Luke, Jesus refused to limit his ministry to his place of birth, but saw himself as a missionary who sought and saved the lost in all communities in the area (Luke 19:10 RSV). In Mark's gospel, Jesus was rejected simply because he was from the family of a carpenter or tradesman. He was identified as Mary's son, implying that Joseph his father was dead, or there remains some suspicion surrounding his birth from a virgin mother. Other family issues of the text have included whether Jesus has any biological brothers and sisters from his mother Mary. Suffice it to say, that Jesus was not being groomed from a priestly family to become a priestly temple authority or prophet in his time. It is similar to man who used to work in the manufacturing company, attending seminary, then wishing to become a pastor in that same community.

This raises the point today of whether or not familiarity breeds discontentment. This was a saying by the Greek storyteller Aesop and later Mark Twain, who used the phrase then added "and children." How many of us have worked in a place and observed that if certain changes were made or if a new piece of equipment was added, things would run much smoother? This person is often ignored. Later, the employer may hire an expensive expert or specialist in the field to come in, who provides the identical solution that the employee has been suggesting for years — but was ignored. This is the prophet without honor.

In this Pentecost season, we as a church are called to explore ways to do ministry in our community as we use the tools, wisdom, and ideas that are within our midst. However, today's text is a sober reminder that it all depends on who is providing the wisdom. If we do not have faith in the person, then they are perceived as less able to do much help and service to the community.

In Season 3 of *Little House on the Prairie*, the episode titled "Little Lost Girl," the little sister Carrie tagged along for a school assignment, but Mary and Laura failed to keep a close eye on her. Their little sister wandered off and fell into an underground mine shaft. The only hope they had of retrieving the little girl was from a drunken mining engineer who knew the coal mines quite well. But his character remained suspect throughout the episode until the little girl was rescued. Quite often until a traumatic event occurs, we might overlook those people within our community who do have abilities to further the mission of our church. Walnut Grove, the little town in the story, did not have faith in the drunken engineer's abilities to save the little girl. However, he later was able to rescue her, which resulted in a happy ending. The town had new faith in this alcoholic mining engineer.

What does faith in Jesus Christ mean for us today? Is Jesus' death and resurrection from the grave enough for us to not only become baptized/converted, but to grow as his disciples? In Mark's gospel, Jesus inaugurates the kingdom of God. To follow him is to be a part of this kingdom. Some commentators observe that possibly his home town of Nazareth wanted a more glorious, visibly supernatural disclosure from God, rather than a regular human such as themselves, whose name is Jesus of Nazareth. For Mark, Jesus became the Messiah as he suffered real human weaknesses, similar to the suffering servant of Isaiah 52-53.

What happens if this suffering servant narrative is not enough? What happens if the home town is expecting a "bigger show?" Some churches might struggle with this even today. Are churches trying to attract people to worship with modern technology tools, and then later informing them that this religion is actually about suffering, sacrifice, and giving oneself up for the benefit of other people as Jesus said in his mission statement in Mark 10:45? ("For the Son of Man also came not to be served but to serve, and to give his life as a ransom for many" Mark 10:45 (RSV). Is any given congregation willing to live with the possibility that people hear the message of a suffering servant Messiah and respond, "Thanks but no thanks... we want something a bit more flashy and glorious?" This is a question that Saint Mark's gospel brings to the table in this lectionary cycle.

Are there more people out there than we realize who really do not want a "human Jesus who suffers" and will therefore resist being his disciples who are called to do the same? This might be a Pentecost season question people of the Christian faith reflect upon. The mission of the church continues in Mark's gospel (Mark 10:45).

Jesus did not allow the rejection of his home town to dissuade him from his mission. He moved onto the commission of his twelve disciples split them into teams of two to carry on a mission to have authority over unclean spirits. He had them travel light. They were not permanent resident priests or clergy. This brought up the idea that a missionary was a temporary presence who was a different ministry than resident pastor, who in that day would be the resident rabbi of the community.

They were to stay at the accommodations offered to them by hosts. They were not to seek a nice hotel or a fancy bed and breakfast with more choices for food and possibly a pool or other accommodations. They were to do their mission and then move on. Most commentators agree that one message the disciples were to preach at this point was to repent, as John the Baptizer also preached (Mark 1:4 RSV). If they were refused, then they were to move on and shake the dust off their feet. This tradition came from a practice of travelling to Gentile lands, then shaking the Gentile dust off their feet before entrance into the Holy Land. It was as if Jesus almost anticipated that his disciples would be rejected just as he was by his home town of Nazareth.

There is some good news for all of us here in church today. Sometimes we can do so much, or at least our very best to help, counsel, suggest, and yes maybe even "preach" a little bit to those whom we love. They may ignore us. Rather than get discouraged, we are called to move on and continue on with the mission God calls us. There are people that even Jesus Christ himself could not reach with his message. Possibly we can view this as a "seed planted," and somebody else must nurture it in other ways.

In the opening illustration, the high school student did take advantage of their school's tutoring services. These are professionals who are extremely patient with slower learners. The math grades did go up significantly! The father was able to take some boys out to his machine shop and show them some operations to build projects on the machine. The pastoral candidate moved onto the next state and was very successful at ministering to people who had similar backgrounds to his family. The other good news here is that God's hand still works mysteriously, even amidst rejections in life. One of the recurring themes of Mark's gospel is that the kingdom of God is a mystery. It begins small and insignificant, as mustard seed, but puts forth the greatest branches much later (Mark 4:30-32 RSV). God continues to meet us when we are rejected. He reminds us that he knows the feeling of rejection — let's take today in Nazareth for example! He points us to new life. This new life takes the form of us being encouraged to carry on because in Mark's gospel the Spirit immediately moves us onto the next chapter of our mission in this season of Pentecost.

Amen.

Sources:

Hugh Anderson, *The New Century Bible: The Gospel of Mark,* (London, UK: Marshall, Morgan and Scott, 1976).

Morna D. Hooker, *Black's New Testament Commentaries: The Gospel According to Mark, 2nd Edition,* (Peabody, MA: Hendrickson Publishers, 1997).

Which Kingdom Do We Serve?

Imagine a middle-sized company or organization who had an upper manager who was soon going to retire. This person's position would need to be replaced. There were workers in the back shop and office areas who would very much like to be considered for this opening position. One particular employee had put in much time and effort in his spare time — even off the clock — to be considered for this position. It was a raise in pay and the worker had been loyal to the company for a number of years. The worker had earned the respect of the fellow workers. This person had gone out of his way to attend seminars and to learn the product as well as the inner operations of the company — from when the product entered the door to when it left on the shipping dock. This person had worked meticulously to learn this position that soon would be vacated. It had taken years, but they believed their time had arrived to move up into a more responsible and higher paying position was due.

At the retirement party of the outgoing manager, the president of the company had a surprise announcement to make. While he knew the person in the company had worked very hard to be considered for the vacant position, he had decided to go in a different direction. His daughter was dating a young man who just graduated from a nearby university. They were engaged to get married. The new position would go to his future son-in-law. The person who had been working hard to earn this promotion may be asked to train this young man for the vacant position.

The worker who had wanted the job decided to speak truth to power. First, this hiring practice used to be called "nepotism," which was unethical. Second, the knowledge of the products and company operations should be the criterion for the new person considered for an upper management position. Third, the workers and other staff would have to get to know this young man who got the job, simply because he was dating the boss' daughter. This lowered the morale in the company because workers realize it was "who you know, not what you know" to get ahead in the company. The seasoned worker who trained for the job did not back down nor apologize for making these arguments. There was tension and friction in the air for the rest of the afternoon.

On Monday morning, this same person was prevented from entering the front door of the company. They were asked to surrender their company ID badge. Their job was terminated! The boss' daughter and her fiancée peeked outside the window to make sure there were no incidents that would entail in calling law enforcement. Life is not fair. Following the rules does not always work. Good people do get hurt for standing up for what they believe to be right. This is also the world in our gospel lesson of the Mark 6 today, as it relates to John the Baptist.

This particular passage is another example of Mark the evangelist "sandwiching" one story within another one. The initial story was Jesus sending out the twelve disciples to do ministry. While they were gone, this account is inserted into Mark, chapter 6. After the story of John the Baptist, the return of the twelve disciples' missionary work was resumed. What point did Mark wish to make here? I believe Mark wanted to challenge us during this season of Pentecost or the church to ask, which kingdom do we serve?

Officially in office, King Herod was the monarch over the people of Judah, though the nation was under Roman Empire occupation. Did Herod serve the kingdom of God instead of the Roman Empire? Secular historian Flavius Josephus wrote in both of his "Antiquities' and *Jewish War* books that the family of King Herod was very deceptive, dysfunctional, and would literally backstab, or kill anyone even within their own bloodline to gain power or monetary advantage. It is contested as to whom in particular King Herod was in this text, but he was a relative of the one who killed the baby boys in Matthew 2.

Herod had married his half-brother's wife Herodias. This was forbidden in Leviticus 18:16. Since he was the monarch over Judah and should have been a role model for living out the Torah, John the Baptist called the king out on this indiscretion. Herod realized that John was probably correct, and also knew the crowds admired John the Baptist. He feared revolution if he took too aggressive a stance in retaliating against John. The crowds realized that John the Baptist was probably the voice in the wilderness spoken of in Malachi 4. Herodias, the wife of Herod, did not like John as he was a possible threat for her quest for power. This was not the first time such a power grab had been attempted in scripture.

All of the commentaries consulted refer to King Ahab's marriage to

Jezebel in 1 Kings 17-18. She tried to promote her false gods of Baal. Elijah the prophet called out both Ahab and Jezebel about this idolatry. Here again was a monarch who was willing to be manipulated by a wife whose intentions were not that of the kingdom of the God of Israel, but for personal gain.

As the story goes in Mark 6, Herod had a wedding banquet and Herodias' daughter entertained the king and his party with a dance. There have been questions about the exact name of this girl. Josephus names her "Salome" and some biblical commentators believe she was named after her mother. She was a product of her mother's first marriage. Her age has been estimated from about twelve to nineteen years old. Her dance impressed Herod so much that he pledged to grant her a promise of her choice. Whether her dance was erotic in nature remains contested but it is not out of the question. Herod had probably had a lot of alcohol to drink and was not making the best judgment calls at that point.

Rather than coming up with a wish on her own in response to King Herod, she went to the side and asked her mother Herodias what would be a good wish. Herodias, still feeling threatened by John the Baptist, who was now imprisoned, told her daughter to request John the Baptist's head on a platter. Before one gets too judgmental of this request, it was common among many army warriors of that time to behead their deceased enemies and plant the head on the fence outside of their homes to indicate their victory.

Another footnote here might be found as far back as in 1 Samuel 17, where young David the shepherd boy cut off the head of Goliath the Philistine upon knocking the giant to the ground with stones from his sling. As this relates to the Mark 6 text, Herodias was now victorious over John the Baptist, the prophet sent from God. John played by the rules. He did what prophets did by confronting the king, and it cost him his life. John chose to serve the kingdom of God rather than the kingdom of Herod's Rome.

In this season of Pentecost what are we as a congregation willing to take risks — even if it means our death? In Mark's gospel, John the Baptist's death would foreshadow Jesus' death on the cross for the sins of humanity. But this kingdom would live beyond any grave and unto eternity. There is new life after every death. This is the good news of the Christian church. Before we take costly risks, we should ask ourselves which kingdom we are serving? The twelve disciples also would soon find out.

When the disciples returned with positive reports of ministry well done, Mark the gospel writer also wanted to warn readers that both Jesus and his disciples of a similar untimely death as that of John the Baptist. This includes us here in our church today. Which kingdom do we serve and to what extent are we willing confront power forces that would threaten our lives as Christians and as a community of faith? Do we serve a kingdom in which it is worth risking and giving our lives? This is a very real and cutting edge question in North America these days when a growing number of people believe they can be spiritual without being associated with any community of faith. Many simply abandon church and organized religion altogether! The kingdom of God that Jesus is ushering in was a threat to so many powerful people in Mark's gospel. Where does this kingdom fit into our priorities? Before we fall into a self-guilt response, let us consider Jesus' disciples in Mark.

Besides following Jesus and carrying out this mission in Mark 6, the disciple grows worse and worse in Mark's gospel. They do not want to believe Jesus when he makes his passion predictions about dying on the cross and rising from the grave three days later (Mark 9:30-32). They really prefer a Messiah of glory, if truth be told. When Jesus was arrested and crucified, all of his disciples abandoned him! Nobody stayed at the foot of the cross. Nobody visited with Jesus on the cross asking him to remember them in his kingdom as Luke's gospel reported. Jesus died alone and did indeed proclaim, "My God, my God, why hast thou forsaken me?" It felt as if God had also forsaken Jesus. Jesus knew what it meant to experience total loneliness, and even the absence of the hand of God.

This same Jesus knows how we feel when we do the right things, and still get abused, suffer the loss of a job, or are abandoned by people whom we thought were our companions. His own disciples had no desire to follow him to the cross! Later in Mark 16:8 during the report of the empty tomb, the women — Mary Magdalene, Salome, and Mary the Mother of James — saw the young man who told them Jesus had risen and to go tell the disciples, yet "they said nothing to anyone, for they were afraid" Mark 16:8(RSV). What is the good news here?

The open-ended conclusion of Mark's gospel allows us to write our own chapter ending of our discipleship journey. Will we meet Jesus to do more mission wherever we identify a Galilee or will we simply live in fear? The good news is God gives us many second chances, even if we fail like the disciples did in Mark's gospel. The other good news is that the Herodias' and King Herod's need not have the last word in our lives if we serve the kingdom of God that John and Jesus preached. In modern terms being told, "You're fired!" need not be the final chapter in our lives. Mark's gospel allows us to write our own endings to the book in our lives.

The fired person in the opening illustration went on to find other employment in another community as a manager. Now he comes to work with his head held high. There is integrity in standing up for what one believes in and taking both the positive and negative consequences for such a thought out position. As workers from the former place of employment grew discontent, they too applied for a position at the company who hired the discharged worker. Mark's gospel provides the choice of either remaining afraid or going on to do mission or ministry elsewhere. This is the kingdom of God we serve on this seventh Sunday after Pentecost.

Amen.

Sources:

M. Eugene Boring, *New Testament Library: Mark,* (Louisville, KY: Westminster John Knox Press, 2006).

Stephen Carter, *Integrity,* (New York: Harper Perennial, 1996).

Adela Yarbro Collins, *Hermeneia: Mark,* (Minneapolis, MN: Fortress Press, 2007).

Morna Hooker, *Black's New Testament Commentaries: The Gospel of St. Mark,* (Peabody, MA: Hendrickson Publishers, 1991).

Gathered Around Jesus

There are both perks and problems for a congregation that is located near a military base. As the families of military personnel are constantly in a state of flux due to assignments and deployments, there are constant rotations of the local population. One particular congregation that worships with less than one hundred people per Sunday was fortunate enough to have three families move into their worship community. This enhanced the ministry of the congregation both in terms of financial giving, volunteers, and encouraged younger people to participate in Christian education ministries. There was both a full time pastor and part time office staff, with plenty of volunteers to help out with music, children's, and stewardship ministries. For a period of three to four years, the ministry was splendid! One could even call it the elusive "plum call" for clergy. However, there were also problems with a church near a base with populations which were in transition.

One hot, humid, August before the beginning of the fall programs, these three families had been reassigned to bases elsewhere. Also, there was another family in the church whose father's business had been sold and he was seeking employment out of state. Now the church was in very anxious times. They felt like the community of Saint Mark's gospel; forces beyond their control were threatening the life of their ministry. The pastor had to seek other employment to supplement his family income. The church office assistant was no longer a paid position. Taking a clue from the gospel lesson today, the church council decided to go away for a weekend and rest, pray, and reflect a while at a retreat house.

They invited a speaker from their judicatory to lead their weekend retreat. The council was told that they were not the only ones who had experienced such a sudden change in both worship and giving numbers. It was happening throughout both mainline and conservative congregations in North America for a variety of demographic and cultural reasons. The church council was given various models of what other churches had experimented with in terms of bi-vocational pastoral ministry, consolidation of congregations, and multiple point parishes (where a pastor serves more than one congregation). Before this conversation took place, the more basic question was how they were to be "gathered around Jesus" as the disciples were doing in today's gospel lesson? Why are we here as community of faith?

In Mark 6, it had not been an easy week for Jesus and the disciples. Jesus was rejected in Nazareth. He did send his disciples on a mission to preach repentance and pray. There was the bad news of John the Baptist's execution after doing faithful ministry. Now there were crowds who followed Jesus and his disciples. Jesus had compassion on them because they were like sheep without a shepherd Mark 6:34 (RSV).

What happens when people experience a sudden change of events that leaves them feeling isolated, lonely, and with fewer resources? Families who had given much time, money, and talents to a given congregation's ministry leave an obvious void, as more pews are empty. The weekly offering was such that the pastor was asked to hold on to his paycheck for another week of offering to cover the amount of the check. It became time to "rest awhile" Mark 6:31 (RSV).

Jesus went away with his disciples and rested awhile. The people continued to come and had endless needs. This is very similar to a person who works in an office or shop who has many assignments and projects to do. All are labeled as: "urgent, immediate attention required, or hot job!" In some organizations, there are people who are the work horses that are willing to bear the brunt of the work assignments and will not leave until they are close to completion. There are others who watch the clock and are out the door when the second hand hits the last hour hand of the day. Jesus and his disciples were in the former group of people. But they also needed their "space."

Regarding the congregation who had the retreat after losing three key families, they broke into "small share groups," they compared notes, they shared what they could glean with the denominational person, and they worshiped and took communion together. They had to reflect and wrestle with the question of what God was calling them to do as they were gathered around Jesus on that day. They took a cue from texts such as Mark 6.

The community was in need of feeding programs. However, not every church could meet every need. Also there were those programs who took government surplus such as cheese, butter, and canned meats, which had to ask for identifications and proof of residency. The church council and pastor decided to coordinate which days of the week other churches and organizations offered food programs. They would offer a children's after-school meal one day a week and possibly volunteer at the community food bank once a month. Did this solve all of their problems? No!

While community people and town officials were glad for this outreach program, it did not translate into either higher church worship attendance, or more financial giving. The church invited twelve-step groups into their building, who were very grateful for the safe place for their loved ones to meet in a church basement. Again, this did not translate into higher worship attendance, or more financial giving. However, like Mark's gospel describing the mustard seed, in Mark 4, the church did have a very real, relevant presence in the community. The denomination knew the congregation was trying and was willing to partner with other forms of ministry in the area. They tried to send out supplies and other preachers to work with the congregation. Would the church die or close its doors?

One of the scholarly issues of Mark's gospel is why Jesus instructed people not to tell anybody what had just occurred. Jesus even did this during the Transfiguration event when Peter, James, and John saw Jesus' appearance change into dazzling white. They were not to tell anybody about this event, until "the Son of Man had risen from the dead" (Mark 9:9). For Mark, Jesus became the Messiah after he died on the cross for the sins of humanity and arose from the grave. For Christians today, what are we called to die for as we gather around Jesus? This is a question that might guide our mission as a church in this season of Pentecost.

In one of the final episodes of "Little House on the Prairie," the townspeople learned that a land development tycoon had acquired the title to all the land in Hero Township or Walnut Grove, which they had believed to be homesteading land. The community leaders failed to defeat the land baron's claim on legal grounds. Finally, the townspeople were inspired by Laura Ingalls Wilder's rage to vent their anger at what they saw as an injustice, so they decided to take a drastic plan of action. Their beloved town of Walnut Grove was laced with sticks of dynamite, as the townspeople decided to blow up the buildings rather than allow them to fall into the hands of a greedy land baron.

When the land baron arrived to claim the town, he found all the town's buildings destroyed. The people of the town left to start new lives elsewhere as many of them had done before. The people marched out of the town singing "Onward Christian Soldiers." As this might relate to Mark's gospel in Mark 16:6-7, the man in the empty tomb told the women to tell the disciples to meet Jesus at Galilee. New ministry could begin there.

Today's gospel lesson begins at Mark 6:30-34 and continues at 6:53-56. The sick, hungry, and needy people did not go away. However, Jesus and his disciples did go onto a boat and travel to other areas. It is not unreasonable to believe that they took time to rest a while. Then they resumed their ministry.

For Christians, we are reminded that we all need a sabbath such as is taught in the ten commandments in Exodus 20:10-11. God wants us to have a day of rest. This is simply not a matter of sitting back and watching television, going to a local sports event, or having a good time. It is intended for us to find ways to gather around our faith in Jesus, as the disciples did in Mark 6.

In this season of Pentecost, the question that congregations and Christians should consider is what it means to gather around Jesus during our down times or times of rest. This is a spiritual question that the Christian church and people of faith are always called to ask. We can wrestle with ideas as we also find ways to become rested, energized, and empowered for the week ahead. Then we are better equipped to do daily ministry with the forms of sick, hungry, and hurting people we find in our lives. It may be our workload at our place of employment. It might be family problems which are under our roof in many forms and now in many age groups.

The teachings such as the ten commandments and sabbath command are given to us as a way of living out a better and more harmonious community life — they not meant to be a burden. Jesus rested as did his disciples. There is a time to stand back and ask why we are doing what we are doing as a Christian, church, and community organization. What are we willing to die on the cross for as Jesus would for the sins of humanity? When is it time to get into the boat and seek out other places to do ministry? Are we willing to live with the possibility of death that Jesus had to keep in his mind? He would indeed die and his disciples would all abandon him and he would be alone on a cross - yet, seeds of the kingdom had been planted along the way.

In this season of Pentecost when many mainline denominational churches wonder about their future, Mark 6 is an invitation for those of us who gather around Jesus to, "Come away to a deserted place all by yourselves and rest awhile" Mark 6:31 (RSV). We may have to live with a very real possibility that congregations will die. But there is new life after every death. What kind of seeds are we planting now? As we gather around Jesus, are we being told what it means to usher in the kingdom of God in our particular community?" We may have to leave our version of "Walnut Grove" in ruins as they did on "*Little House on the Prairie.*" Also, we may have found new life in our community that differs from that in the past. The good news, which need not burden us, is that our congregation remains Christ's church to gather and scatter.

Amen.

Sources:

Daniel J. Harrington S.J., Sacra Pagina: *The Gospel of Mark,* (Collegeville, MN: The Liturgical Press, 2002).

Morna Hooker, *Black's New Testament Commentaries: The Gospel of St. Mark,* (Peabody, MA: Hendrickson Publishers, 1991).

The Loaves

One of the hardest lessons in life I had to learn was never to get a job at the restaurant I enjoyed eating in since childhood. There was a particular fast food restaurant that had plenty of vegetables and condiments on their sandwiches that I had always looked forward to eating since I was twelve years old. When I got out of college in the 1970s, the job market in my area had a glut of four-year college degree graduates. I applied for a manager trainee position at the restaurant I have cherished since childhood. I was sent to manager training sessions and worked at a training store in a metro area. It was an unforgettable experience. I wondered why God would allow me to do such a thing.

After the novelty of eating sandwiches for a discounted price wore off, I learned about the inner workings of the cooking process for sandwiches, deep fried grease products, and drinks. I also soon learned that the employees there were all working for minimum wage and were unhappy because they were working so hard for low pay. All workers had perpetual applications in other places of employment to get a job with more pay. Training workers for both the kitchen and front counter duties was a perpetual merry-go-round. I learned that other restaurant managers had their "favorite" and not so favorite employees. Restaurant work is hard, long hours. Being on salary as an assistant manager consumed so many hours and weekends, that when I did the math, I was making below minimum wage! My innocence was lost!

Weekends involved long lines of customers who had varying degrees of intoxication that resulted in fistfights and brawling in the lobby. These people were not very friendly like on the TV commercials. Quite often they were more than ready to start a brawl, which resulted in flashing blue lights from local police squad cars in the parking lot. This also scared away customers. When a sudden crowd "rush" occurred after a concert or sports event, there were certain shortcuts in the kitchen that one had to resort to in making the sandwiches, fried products, and dispensing the drinks. I had never known of this reality. It was sort of like being immersed in the unknown world or "Matrix" movie where one would learn they would rather prefer to live in the disillusioned world than that of seeing how this food was really prepared. However, I learned much about food hygiene, how to deal with bottlenecks of long lines of people, as well as waiting for food to be fully cooked and how to deal with people who have short tempers. I learned how to schedule workers on varying shifts as well as how to count and deposit money, receipts, and coupons. But this was not enough for me.

One weekend, I was overscheduled and slept in on Monday morning. The supervising manager called my house and yelled at my mother who picked up the phone. He cursed at her. When I got to the restaurant, he had slammed the phoned down so hard, he had broken it! I thought to myself, "Do I want to give my life to the cause of fast food? Why did God allow me to be here?" I called my college placement center and got an office position in a nearby city. I could not ever eat at one of those restaurants for over ten years. I would make a bologna sandwich and bowl of soup instead. The restaurant meal is not the loaves of bread I desired.

Jesus offers loaves of bread that point to a divine reality beyond any time of hunger or chaos we can ever experience here on this world. In Bible times, before that of refrigeration and electric food storage technology, a typical family spent half of their day getting enough food for meals for just that day. The food had to be consumed at the meal. There were no leftovers to put in the microwave. Barley bread was preferred because the barley ripened before wheat for bread did. Poor people used barley bread as a staple food of the time along with fish that would be smoked similar to how we might eat hard sticks of beef jerky today. Jesus was on top of a mountain in this text. He might be likened to another Moses-like prophet mentioned in Deuteronomy 18:15-18.

Jesus was similar to a prophet such as Elisha in 2 Kings 4:42-44, who fed one hundred people. In John's gospel, many of Jesus' signs or miracles occured around the traditional Jewish festival days, however Jesus fulfilled them in a greater manner. This resulted in hostility from the traditional Judean leaders, which escalated into Jesus' eventual crucifixion in John 18. His death would be for the sins of humanity, so we may eternal life John 3:16 (RSV). In this case, the Passover event celebrated the nation of Israel being delivered from the Egyptians by escaping through the parting of the waters of the Red Sea, and then they were sustained in the desert by eating manna and quail provided by God (Exodus 16; Numbers 11). Jesus' loaves of bread sign "upped the ante" in John 6 in terms of him being more than a Moses prophetic figure.

After observing the large crowds who were hungry, he knew what he was going to do, but decided to test his disciples by asking, "Where are we to buy bread for these people to eat?" John 6:5 (RSV). John was unique to other gospels in that he featured the disciples Andrew and Philip in his stories, rather than Peter, James, and John in the synoptic gospels. Lesser known names do have a place in the kingdom in John's gospel. There was an unnamed boy with five loaves of barley bread and two fish. Jesus took his offering. He had the disciples seat the people in groups of fifty. Jesus then parted the food and fed five thousand people. All four of the gospels report this miracle or sign of feeding five thousand people with bread and fish. John added the details of "barley" bread.

There was enough food that the people were satisfied. Some might have gone back for "seconds," like an all-you-can-eat dinner bar. Jesus told the disciples to gather the food up, "that nothing be lost" (John 6:12). Unlike the manna and quail while in the wilderness under Moses, this food did not perish immediately. Jesus' loaves of bread were to be preserved and served to other people. This could be cross referenced into John 10:10, where Jesus "came that people may have life and have it abundantly." Abundant in this reference is both a quality and quantity of life, which is forward moving (from the Greek word *zway,* where we get the female name Zoey). Jesus was more than a prophetic figure of Moses; he was a Messiah who brought one eternal life (John 3:16 is another cross reference here). Once food had been given, John wished to make another point why Jesus was beyond Moses, as it related to chaos and disorder in peoples' lives. The text continued.

During the walking on the Sea of Galilee at night, John wished to remind people that water represented chaos and disorder in the Hebrew Bible (Old Testament). The event occured at night or during the hours of darkness, which intensified this sense of disorder in John (consider Nicodemus visiting Jesus at night in John 3).

In John's gospel, Jesus is God in the flesh. Jesus was the organizing principle of the universe, also called the "logos." John 1:1-14 is a bold in-breaking beginning or prologue of the gospel. We can have confidence that God has a plan for his people despite the forces of darkness and disorder. Jesus' walking on the Sea of Galilee made this point. Any person of faith could end up working for a restaurant or public place where crowds and lines of people can be as disorienting as the disciples felt here in John 6. John's gospel wished to remind us that God still is there in the person of Jesus or God in the flesh. God remains with us in these times of disorder. There is the promise of deliverance and new life.

More good news of this text today includes that God provides for all of our needs. Whether one works in a chaotic restaurant, office, or public place, we can confidently pray, "Thy kingdom come, thy will be done, on earth as it is in heaven. Give us this day our daily bread," Matthew 6:10-11 (RSV). The feeding of the five thousand resulted in more than enough food. Jesus' walking on the sea of Galilee at night reminds us that there is no event or time of lack or survival resources and no chaos that might invade our lives that Jesus cannot and will not overcome. Furthermore, Jesus pointed us to new life. In the season of Pentecost, what are areas where our congregation might observe we are short of resources? What forces of weather, political seasons, or economic trends might cause us to become frightened? John 6 allows us to go to sleep confident that Jesus provided enough loaves of bread for us to have life and have it abundantly. God still watches over us into the future and for eternity.

After five years, I grew weary of working in an office at an area manufacturer. My wife and I were quite active in our inner city church congregation and I had felt the urge to explore the possibility of being called into the ordained ministry. After many denominational hoops to jump through and probationary acceptance into the seminary (I needed to take Greek and I did poorly on the standard tests), I eventually moved into another state to attend seminary. For a ministry related work study job, I was a supervisor at a church sponsored rescue mission for the homeless and transients in the inner-city.

All of a sudden, the epiphany lights went on for me! I realized that the fast food management training months at the fast food restaurant chain had prepared me for this very position. There were loud, smelly, half-inebriated homeless people who demanded meals and coffee. There were times we had to call the local police when somebody brought a weapon into the mission. The working staff was both fellow seminarians as well as homeless shelter volunteers with varying days of sobriety under their belt.

We all had to think on our feet in food preparation in the event that the church that had signed up to provide food for the evening did not arrive or they had forgot. There were many short-fused tempered people. There were also thankful people who praised God for such a mission. We were fortunate to have generous donors and people of good faith who wished to help in this ministry. If the cook drank too much and relapsed in alcoholic consumption, the mission staff had to improvise. After all, there are one hundred hungry people in the chapel area awaiting a meal after the church service. As one mission staff member, guess who also had to lead worship and preach a sermon on short notice? I still do not eat at the fast food restaurant I worked at. But a good bologna sandwich, bowl of soup, and cup of coffee often hits the spot as one of Jesus' loaves used to feed the five thousand people. How are we as a congregation providing loaves in our community? This is a question to grow on during the season of Pentecost.

Amen.

Sources:

Culpepper, R. Alan, *Intepreting Biblical Texts: The Gospel and Letters of John,* (Nashville, TN: Abingdon Press, 1998).

Lincoln, Andres T. *Black's New Testament Commentary: The Gospel According to Saint John,* (Peabody, MA: Hendrickson Publishers, 2006).

O'Day, Gail R., and Susan E. Haylen, *Westminster Bible Companion: John,* (Louisville, KY: Westminster John Knox Press, 2006).

More Than Gimmicks

A medium-sized congregation with deep northern European roots was located in a college town. The members wanted to attract more college students to their church for weekly worship attendance and other activities. They received a few boxes of donated modern English New Testament books. The intention was to pass them out to the college students on the campus nearby. Besides placing a slip of paper in each New Testament with the church name and address on it, they also placed a coupon for a dollar or even maybe a five dollar in random copies of the New Testament. One could call this a "gimmick" to get younger people to attend church if they knew they could get cash as they redeem this certificate. In other settings such the John 6 text today, it could be viewed as free bread or manna from heaven.

In John 6, Jesus had just fed five thousand people, with leftover food. However, he wished to make the point that this was more than just a gimmick of giving out free food. In today's lesson, crowds of people sought out Jesus again after the first meal, for the wrong reason. One way to understand the entire gospel of John is through the lens of John 10:10, "The thief comes only to steal and kill and destroy; I came that they may have life and have it abundantly John 10:10 (RSV)." The Greek word for life here is *zway*, or forward moving existence that begins today and continues on unto eternity. In short, this life is more than survival. Jesus wanted to provide life.

In John's gospel Jesus invited people into a relationship with him, the Father, and the Holy Spirit. Such a relationship is not simply learning how to say the right things, or confessing the right words, though that is not mutually exclusive to this life. In the epistles of John, the elder reminded believers that one has to confess that Jesus is the Son of the Father 1 John 2:18-28 (RSV). The symbol of "bread" is another metaphor for Jesus in John's gospel.

Roman Catholic theologians are quick to point out that Jesus' giving of his body in the form of bread mirrors the practice of Eucharist or Holy Communion in the church. John does not have a "last supper" meal before Jesus' crucifixion, however this John chapter 6 set of texts lays out a pretty solid foundation that Jesus had intended to use bread as a metaphor for his life that he gave for the sins of humanity, that all of us may have life and have it abundantly now John 3:16-17; 10:10 (RSV).

So where is the "rub?" In this text, the crowds were products of their time and sought daily food for survival and sustenance. Since Jesus had fed them earlier, they opted to come back to Jesus for more bread. It would be like students in the opening illustration redeeming their coupons for a dollar bill, then returning to the same church the next week expecting still another dollar bill. Jesus' response was that the the dollar bill would not last long, just like the bread he had just given the crowds would eventually perish John 6:27 (RSV). Jesus encouraged them to seek the food that that never perished. It is the food that endures to eternal life. The crowds still did not get it. They thought they needed to perform works for this food that endured eternally. Jesus responded that God wished them to believe in the one whom he had sent, that being Jesus as the Messiah. The crowd wanted what would be seen today as "proof" or another magic act or gimmick.

This is why some clergy do not like doing entertainment or tricks up in the pulpit during Sunday sermons. Once a pastor pulls one rabbit out of the hat, the crowds want a bigger rabbit pulled out the hat next week. So many clergy simply opt out, and often state this on their mobility form profiles when they seek another congregation. If certain words such as maybe "transformation, vibrant, or innovative" do not appear on a particular pastoral candidate's profile, the name is put aside by both the judicatory and congregation call committee. Jesus was not willing to do another food miracle or sign, which was not then, nor now, a crowd pleaser to get people into the pews. Instead, Jesus offered a word that was much more potent and contained much more richness. In some denominations, the pastor's official position title is, "Minister of Word and Sacrament." It is not community organizer, entertainer, or activities director.

The crowds appealed to the narrative that Moses was able to provide manna for the people of Israel while they were in the wilderness. This is indeed true. Jesus responded by reminding the people that it was God who provided such manna and quail during the wilderness journey. This bread soon perished. If the nation tried to preserve the food, it would spoil or grow bad while out in the desert's dry lands. Jesus' bread from the past meal was able to be gathered up and given to other people in need. It had a longer shelf life — possibly eternal. "Bread" is a metaphor used by John the evangelist to invite the hungry and thirsty crowds to build a relationship with Jesus, who is God in the flesh John 1:1-14 (RSV).

While Moses' bread was instrumental in delivering the people from Egyptian bondage, they would still die a natural death. Jesus' bread delivered humans from the ultimate enemy, that being death and the grave. This is the good news of the Christian gospel John 3:16-17 (RSV). To be viewed as a credible God-sent leader, there was to be a "deliverer." Moses delivered the people from political intruders and destroyers of life here on earth, just as Christ delivered us from the threat of death, and all that represents death in our lives in the forms of many losses. This might include loss of: employment, property, family members, economic security, and finally despair of feeling our lives lack any meaning beyond our grace. Jesus delivers each of us from these threats today. We are reminded of this when we partake in the communion meal in our church. We are all recipients of God's grace and new life at the communion table.

What else is a "disciple" in John's gospel? Jesus was on the forefront of healing people of many types of illness. To Lazarus who died, he reminded Martha, "I am the resurrection and the life; he who believes in me, though he die, yet shall he live," John 11:25 (RSV). Jesus knew that Judas would betray him, but this did not detract Jesus from staying focused on his mission. Jesus washed his disciples' feet as an example of service to other people John 13 (RSV). Jesus promised the Holy Spirit who would teach his disciples everything John 14:25-26; 16:12-14 (RSV). Jesus anticipated difficult times for his disciples. He left the disciples with the words of, "I have said this to you, that in me you may have peace. In the world you have tribulation; but be of good cheer, I have overcome the world" John 16:33 (RSV). What does this mean for our church today?

People do come to church to see and experience Jesus' care and compassion. In the opening illustration, many college students did return their coupons for the dollar bills. They were also welcomed by church people of all ages. The students were asked to share their concerns, problems, and worries. The students were invited to church members' homes for a meal in the future. The students were given phone numbers to call in the event they were lonely or were anxious about something, since it was the first time away from home for many of them.

As this relates to our congregation, once a person enters into the doors of our church building — regardless of whether it was a gimmick, program, musical event, or free meal that attracted them, how are we showing them how we live out our discipleship as Jesus' disciples? This is a Pentecost season challenge. No amount of a denominational, local festival event or ideas we might have picked up on social media will make people feel as if this could be their church home if we do not do more than give out one bread meal for survival. How are we as a fellowship of Christians showing in our words and action that we do enjoy and share the confidence, nurture and care Jesus the Good Shepherd in John 10?

A concluding story goes like this in my youth memory: My uncle was a not a great church attendee, however, my aunt was quite meticulous in her worship habits. She prayed from her devotional books often three times a day. When her health made driving impossible for her to get to mass, my uncle felt obliged to chauffeur her. He wanted to drop her off at the church then go to the local bar or tavern. One day, he dropped her off and the church custodian motioned my uncle to come into the custodian's back room. There the custodian broke open a case of beer and they sat beside the brooms, vacuum cleaners, and dust pans as they listened to Catholic mass over the loudspeaker that was piped into the custodian's room. My uncle experienced Christ in an unusual but welcoming way. He returned to church again, and again! My uncle and aunt were both major financial givers to the parish. They participated in at least four or five major parish activities every year. The priest knew about this little get together. However, when parish cleaning day occurred, my uncle was right there cleaning, sweeping, and refinishing the sanctuary woodwork. The church sanctuary cleaning event began on Saturday at 9:00 a.m., and they were promptly finished and cracking a twelve-pack open by noon. In my youth then, I often asked myself, "What would Jesus say?"

Amen.

Sources:

R. Alan Culpepper, *Interpreting Biblical Texts: The Gospel and Letters of John,* (Nashville, TN: Abingdon Press, 1998).

Daniel J. Harrington, S.J., *Sacra Pagina: The Gospel of John,* (Collegeville, MN: The Liturgical Press, 1998).

Gail R. O'Day, and Susan E. Haylen, *Westminster Bible Companion: John*, (Louisville, KY: Westminster John Knox Press, 2006).

D. Moody Smith, *Abingdon New Testament Commentaries: John* (Nashville, TN: Abingdon Press. 1999).

Bread And Call

Whenever my wife sends me to the store to buy a loaf of bread, I have to make a difficult decision as to what kind of bread. It depends where we are on our life journey at any given time. For example, while we lived in more urban areas with many bakery shops and stores, I would often purchase fresh bakery bread. It is softer, tastes fresher, and often has many varieties like sourdough, muffin, or cracked wheat bread. The down side of such fresh breads is they have a shorter shelf life and must be consumed within a matter of days before green mold appears on the crusts of the bread. Living in a rural area means purchasing other types of bread.

Since we have had to drive thirty minutes to an hour to the nearest grocery store, I then buy the nationally advertised factory made brands, or the store's "generic" breads. Though I am bread squeezer who tries to determine the softer loaves (usually stacked way in the back of the shelves), because such bread has a longer shelf life of a matter of weeks, but does not taste as fresh. Mold does not appear until about a month has passed. The kind of bread I purchase is determined by the proximity of the grocery store I am near — depending where I live. The bread still gives us life. The bread is still available, but in many varieties. Jesus uses the metaphor of "being the living bread that came down from heaven." He was talking about his calling as the "Messiah or Christ." Jesus knew his calling, here in John 6. We read about it as early as John 1:1-14. How do we know our calling that helps us put bread on the table throughout our lives?

My brother Anthony (named changed for privacy), knew his calling in life since childhood. My dad could not leave any screwdrivers, pliers, or other tools around the house because Anthony would take such tools and disassemble the kitchen toaster, the old television set with many tubes, or the doorknobs in all the rooms. We knew he was going to be a mechanic of some sort, because he had a natural ability to use tools and fix objects. We knew he would not be an electrician because he stuck the screwdriver into the wall socket and was thrown across the room with the electric shock. For Anthony, he only needed to be able to read well enough to decipher machine manuals and assembly directions. He went to the local vocational high school and became a heavy equipment mechanic for thirty years at a manufacturing company, then retired early on in life. Anthony still fixes peoples' cars in his garage in his spare time. His calling gives life to people who need to have mechanical vehicles and machines fixed. At night, he can lay back with a favorite drinking beverage, knowing he has fulfilled his calling in life. It is not so easy with other people such as me. Being "called" into ministry was not so easy for me.

As I take a poll of my clergy colleagues, almost all of them were identified early in life by their pastor, a parochial school teacher or religious matriarch or patriarch in the family to "consider becoming an ordained pastor?" They were the acolyte or altar boy (girls did not consider ministry then in my community, unless they were Roman Catholic, and went to a convent). These young men were steered toward their church's college that prepared them for pastoral ministry and they were later to attend seminary. Very often they played a musical instrument and could lead the congregation in worship with their piano or guitar playing. Their call to ministry was strongly confirmed by their family and friends. I had no such experience, theophany, or Martin Luther event where I was almost struck by lightning until I promised God I would be a monk.

In our lesson today, the Jewish temple leaders complained that Jesus said, "I am the bread which came down from heaven" John 6:41 (RSV). Jesus was identified as "the son of Joseph, whose father and mother we know? How did he then say, 'I have come down from heaven'?" John 6:42 (RSV). Luke's gospel provides the only account of Jesus' childhood at age twelve. Most scholars believe that John had access to the same sources that Mark had about Jesus. In Mark 6:1-6, Jesus was identified as the "carpenter, the son of Mary" Mark 6:3 (RSV). He was a tradesman or skilled worker, not trained temple rabbi. He was not groomed for seminary.

Using bread as a metaphor, Jesus affirmed he was the word made flesh stated in John 1:14. Other known forms of bread such as that provided in the wilderness in Exodus 16, also resulted in the people murmuring that they were dissatisfied. Walter Brueggemann, the Hebrew Bible author, makes this point in the *"Theology of the Old Testament"* volume that the desire or temptation to return to Egypt with both its fleshly pleasures along with heavy burdens rather than survive in the wilderness has always been a temptation for the people of faith. It is similar to a person reminiscing about the "good old days" of their youth, while blocking out the dark times and burdens that prompted them to want move on with their lives. In this sense, scripture remains a living word for us even today.

The bread Jesus wishes to offer is that which provides eternal life. Jesus was using bread a metaphor for his own body being offered up as on a cross in John 18-19. In John, Jesus' crucifixion was his hour, for which he was willing to be the final Passover lamb for the sins of humanity. John's gospel often uses the Jewish festivals as a literary tool to show how Jesus more than fulfilled the meaning of a particular festival such as Passover. His calling was to die for the sins of humanity so that we might have eternal life. John 3:16 summarized this calling, "For God so loved the world that he gave his only Son, that whoever believes in him should not perish but have eternal life" John 3:16 (RSV).

John's gospel challenges us to explore what calling we have, one which we are willing to die for, that also points us beyond this life. This is a Pentecost question for both the church as a group and us as individual Christians. This is part of the life journey and may change, just as my decisions as to which kind of bread to purchase is at the store.

In my case, I was never slated to attend college while in high school. I was at the lower fifth of my class in high school. I was not good in gym class either, so the military was out for me. I ended up in the same vocational school as my brother Anthony; however, they only had openings in "Printing and Graphic Arts." So I attended that vocational school for two years.

While I was not viewed as an academic scholar in my suburban high school, I was at the top of the class among the urban students in my vocational school printing class. One student per year was chosen to attend a state college which taught printing, and I was chosen. I worked hard on the hot metal type and photo typesetting equipment, estimating printing jobs and planning production schedules which they had at that time. I graduated with "Distinction", with a bachelor's degree in printing management. Eventually, I found myself working in an urban envelope manufacturing company for a few years. It was an "okay" job. It was low paying compared to the major manufacturing companies in the area. I concluded at age 29, that I did not want to give my life to the printing industry.

I saw skilled machine pressmen lose their fingers. I saw plant managers smoke and drink alcohol to the point of an early grave. This was my "manna" in the wilderness. My wife and I were very active in our local urban church. It got to the point where I lived for weekends at church and dreaded my office desk at work. With my pastor and congregation's support, I applied to the judicatory to be considered for seminary. After about a year worth of tests, exams, and interviews, I was told that I could apply for one of the denomination's seminaries. Since I went to a trade college, I was placed on "probation" for a year at seminary and had to take extra classes in New Testament Greek and Theological Reading. Seminary was challenging, hard, and life changing. This is for another sermon. However, I found my calling in life as a "pastor" for small town and rural congregations. If I died and Jesus took me up on the last day and told me he had a congregation in a rural setting for me on some other planet or galaxy, I could live with this for eternity.

My brother could not live eternally with the automotive shop vocation, as he enjoyed his outdoor garden. For him working in the garden from dawn to dusk, despite the bugs and mosquitos was heaven on earth. He lived his life in a dirty auto factory, so his children could onto to college to find vocations of their liking. I think my wife would love working at a pet shelter for eternity. It is where she sees life eternal. This is the bread that feeds her soul.

On this day, Jesus offers his life as bread for each of us here to have life and have it abundantly in both a time here on earth and a quality of life. The good news for each of us here today is Jesus offers us new life in his death and sacrifice so we will be raised on the last day John 6:44 (RSV). We all are invited to share our faith journey that leads us to a particular calling which we may or may not be able to earn a living doing.

I am reminded of a parishioner who worked in a rock quarry all of his life to support his wife with many illnesses, as well as his children. He was good at working with wood and his hands. Upon retirement, he made our church its "crucifer's cross" that still stands in the church sanctuary. He refinished the church baptismal font and built a small wooden altar table for the church worship book up rest upon. These are symbols of the faith that point people to the new life we all share with Jesus the Christ as our bread in life.

Amen.

Sources:

Walter Brueggemann, *Theology of the Old Testament: Testimony, Dispute, Advocacy,* (Minneapolis, MN: Augsburg Fortress Press, 2012).

Ruth B. Edwards, *Discovering John: Content, Interpretation, Reception,* (Grand Rapids, MI: Wm. B. Erdmann's, 2003).

Daniel J. Harrington, S.J., *Sacra Pagina: The Gospel of John,* (Collegeville, MN: The Liturgical Press, 1998).

D. Moody Smith, *Abingdon New Testament Commentaries: John,* (Nashville, TN: Abingdon Press. 1999).

Proper 15 / Ordinary Time 20 / Pentecost 12
John 6:51-58

Belonging At The Table

Have you ever had a "bad communion experience in church?" I sure did, when I was told that my employer was no longer able to pay me and I needed to seek a position elsewhere. I was broken. This was also my source of medical insurance and housing provisions. Being a long time Christian of faith, I attended a Saturday night worship service at a local church. They were to serve Holy Communion that evening. I asked the clergyman if I could take communion. Once I told him my denomination, he told me he would rather I not take communion in their congregation because he was not sure I really believed the way they did about the body and blood of Jesus Christ. I was crushed! First, I was suddenly out of a job. I thought the first place to seek refuge was the church or as I was taught, "God's house." Second, since childhood I was taught no matter how bad things get in life, would I have a place at the table of the Lord in the Jesus' church. A couple who were laity overheard my conversation with the pastor. They both gently placed their hands on my shoulder and invited me into another room. There, they talked with me and prayed with me.

I thanked them for their care and loving presence. However, I also reminded them that my story is another one of those negative experiences that people share about "church." When my wife and family hear about this, the story will spread like wildfire in a dry grass mountain forest. Unfortunately, the good charity and mission work will not be as well-known as my relatives all sharing church stories over a few drinks, "Our brother-in-law was turned away from this particular church for communion, after he had lost his job. What kind of God do they worship there?" While I see myself as loyal to the church to the point of seeking out another congregation, there are other people in our family who simply joined the growing numbers of "none and done" with organized religion in America. This sort of story is keeping it real for future church trends in America.

I did return to another church. I was welcomed at their communion table and continued to worship by giving offerings to their World

Mission Relief Fund. Unfortunately, the question of who belongs at the communion table remains a sticking point in some churches. Giving to the offering and participating in communion is my way of abiding in Jesus the true vine, another metaphor John's gospel used in John 15. In this Pentecost season, today's text serves as reminder about participating in Jesus as the flesh and blood that leads to eternal life John 6:54 (RSV).

At first glance, this particular text appears to be speaking of cannibalism, which evoked feelings of disgust in much of the Mediterranean world of that time. However, Jesus was referring to the Exodus 16 and Numbers 20 accounts of God's providing for the people of Israel being fed while wandering in the wilderness. God provided quail and manna for the people after their cries to God for food, after being delivered from Egyptian bondage. In the Old Testament or Hebrew Bible, "salvation" means to be delivered from some less than desirable situation. While Moses delivered the people from the Egyptian Pharaoh, Jesus in John had something far more comprehensive in mind.

In John, when Jesus died on the cross for the sins of humanity, it is on the exact Passover day. The synoptic gospels place the last supper on Passover day, whereas John placed Jesus' crucifixion on that same day. Jesus is the final Passover Lamb that was used to deliver people from political bondage. However, Jesus' sacrifice was intended to deliver humanity from sin and death. To have a relationship with Jesus is to have eternal life and they will be lifted up on the last day from their graves John 6:54 (RSV). How does one know if they are in right relationship with this Jesus as Messiah who is God in the flesh? John 1:1-14 (RSV).

"He who eats my flesh and drinks my blood abides in me, and I in him" John 6:56 (RSV). When I was turned away from the communion table in the opening illustration, I felt as if I no longer belonged to this larger body in Jesus Christ. I felt as if I was not part of the vine in John 15. I had been baptized, attended church, even been ordained as a pastor, but was refused at the communion table. The time that I needed to feel God's grace and presence the most, was when it was denied. Again, I persisted and found another congregation. However, today as such stories as mine are shared and there are people who are less patient with the church and simply will drop being part of organized religion totally. Do we need requirements for who partakes in the Holy Communion? In my years of ministry, I have seen the answer to this question evolve.

When I was ordained in my denomination in the 1980s, "First Communion" was usually given at the age of confirmation, or at affirming one's baptismal vows. This seemed to be etched in "stone" where I served as a pastor. Slowly, it became apparent that many people might have been baptized, but never confirmed for many legitimate reasons. An example might be a child who was embarrassed to attend both school and church classes because their family's name was in the local newspapers as related to a crime that was playing itself out very slowly in the court system. An Adult Inquirers Class might be useful for the child to learn more about the church's views on scripture, sacraments/rites, and so on. This becomes a "win-win" solution for both the family and the congregation who wants to maintain some sort of standards for first communion.

In some church traditions, it is a practice to have first communion classes and then the child takes first communion around fifth grade. This is whenever the parents and sponsors deem it a good age for the child to recognize what the communion meal entails for their faith and life of the church. It is a matter of belonging to a community of faith which sustains a person regardless of how successful they are; financially viable or what sort of physical or mental illness they have may have.

There was once a young lady who had tourette's syndrome — with outbursts of uncontrollable language and foul words — who came to worship at a church while she was away at college. The pastor called her home congregation. They were confident that this lady was fully committed to the Christian faith! She was very intelligent. She actually had two college majors. When her outbursts occurred, people would usher her into the narthex until she was finished. They would also offer her the communion meal, if such an outburst occurred during the communion portion of the service. According to John 6, she still eats Jesus' flesh and drinks his blood and has eternal life. This is the nature of grace! We do not find God, but God finds us, just as he did the people who were in bondage to Egypt in the book of Exodus and in whatever forms of bondage we might have today! The body and blood of our Lord is given for each of us whose faith is in the crucified and risen Lord Jesus Christ. This is a basic Christian message which the church can share today. In times when people are often measured by their looks, first impressions, how their employment resume appears, they still belong to the table which shares the body and blood of our Lord Jesus Christ. This is the gospel of the Christian church!

Today the communion meal is part of ingesting a real symbol and for many churches, a sacrament or means of grace which assures us of eternal life. When do we take communion? I believe we take it regularly and especially when we feel least worthy of it! This is when we need to feel and experience God's gracious love through the body and blood of our Lord the most.

Rather than get bogged down in the words related to flesh, blood, and possible implied cannibalism, I believe John wanted to provide readers that "…these are written that you may believe that Jesus is the Christ, the Son of God, and that believing you may have life in his name" John 20:31 (RSV). It is not a matter of getting words right but belonging at the table of the one who wishes to give us life and give it abundantly John 10:10 (RSV).

Amen.

Sources:

Daniel J. Harrington, S.J., *Sacra Pagina: The Gospel of John,* (Collegeville, MN: The Liturgical Press, 1998).

Craig S. Keener, The Gospel of John: A Commentary, Volume one, (Peabody. MA: Hendrickson Publishers LLC., 2003).

Gail R. O'Day, and Susan E. Haylen, *Westminster Bible Companion: John,* (Louisville, KY: Westminster John Knox Press, 2006).

Lord To Whom Shall We Go?

Despite his best efforts at teaching, feeding, and healing, today Jesus is rejected. However, he is still our Lord. This is good news for us today.

A pastor was about to attend a book fair in a neighboring county and was getting ready to leave the church office. It was early after lunch on a summer afternoon. A young man in his late twenties and his little one-year-old daughter suddenly walked into the pastor's office, and crashed down in the chair in front of the pastor's desk. The young man was noticeably shaken. The little girl was running around the office and in and out of the doors of other rooms. The man announced that his wife wanted a divorce! They had been married for less than a year, and this pastor performed both the premarital counseling and wedding service. The young man said that he had tried his best to keep the marriage together.

Their differences were in financial philosophy, which the pastor had warned the couple about earlier. The wife liked to spend the limits of many credit cards, while floating the outstanding overdue payments — and then got even more credit cards. When she was in trouble, she called her mother to help out financially. On the other hand, the husband was a spend thrift. He had one credit card which he kept an eagle eye on the spending daily. He was careful about every dollar that came in and out of the household. He liked to shop at the less expensive stores, whereas she enjoyed the higher end, brand named stores. The couple went to financial counseling with their accountant. Both had careers that they enjoyed. Both had experienced higher education degrees and believed they were on their way to the American dream. Yet it had all come to a screeching halt!

The young father and husband sat in the pastor's office and expressed the pleading words of, "how to make this pain go away." He felt rejected. Since his high school championship sports days, he was used to setting goals, measuring their steps to completion, and then accomplishing these goals in a timely if not record setting manner that resulted in a trophy, medal, or ribbon for his showcase of awards. Now he was being told his wife wanted out of the marriage. His best efforts were not good enough! What was next for this young man and daughter?

The pastor visited the wife and she had indeed announced that she wanted out of the marriage. No amount of counseling or talking would convince her otherwise. Her mother interrupted the conversation and bid the pastor farewell. The mother said she would handle her daughter's grief and other problems within their own household.

The young man went to his friends at work with similar stories of broken marriages. They sat in the local bars and shared their own personal stories. The young man attended worship at the church with his daughter. He wondered what he did wrong in the marriage. Up to this point in his life he had been a scholarship college recipient and champion college athlete winner of multiple trophies — he had never experienced this kind of rejection in his entire life. This began a long two-year court trauma with fights over custody and child support. It entailed expensive court fees, legal costs, bitter words spoken on both sides, along with weekend conflicts over visitation privileges with their daughter. Many days were spent with his close friends as he told the same sad story many times. However, he realized he needed to get on with life, despite this rejection during the messy divorce. He did not want to find himself sitting at a local bar sharing the same stories as many of his friends were doing. He tried to take his Christian faith seriously — despite lapses in church attendance. John's gospel has good news for such people.

Some scholars believe that John the evangelist wrote his gospel to a church that was rejected from the Jewish temple after 85 CE, in one of the Jewish councils of Jamnia that classified the Christians as "heretics" (Martin, 56). One could easily use the metaphor that it was a messy divorce of sorts. It might explain why John's gospel has the distinction of being particularly critical of Jews. The modern scholarly way to avoid anti-Semitism (I have read) is to call the "Jews" either temple leaders or Judeans. However, like the young couple getting divorced, the bitterness and hurt lingers on for many months, if not years. So how do we find good news and life in this gospel? What is this life?

The New Testament has three words for life that are commonly used. *Psuche* (psyche) life such as is in Matthew 16:25, refers to life as inner being or soul. That is a person who wants to save his life, but in doing so could lose his soul. We get the world "psychology" from this word. Next, there is the "bios" life, meaning the physical formation of life where we get the words biology and biography. Luke 8:14 refers to this life as the sower of a plants' new life in the form of seeds. John 6 refers to *zoe* or *zway* life which is vigorous, active, or added from above sort of life. The *asch* form of life has legitimate uses in scripture and in personal Christian living (Neumann, 79).

For example, a person whose life has been shattered and disorganized or is recovering from upheaval might want to settle down and form a new contour or create a stable shape in life. This might be a "bios" form of life. They wish to organize their lives similar to a biographical sketch. On the other hand, a person who has suffered trauma and violation of personal boundaries may seek a *psyche* or inner healing of the soul. Here in John's gospel, the writer liked the Greek term, *zway* or *zoe*, which is a forward moving, vibrant life. God meets us in difficult circumstances and then points us to move ahead in our life journey. There is no bad situation that we cannot move beyond with this *zway* or *zoe* life. There are other examples in John's gospel.

In John 14, Jesus met a Samaritan woman at the water well who had had five husbands and was living with a man who was not her husband. Yet, Jesus promised her eternal life that was the *zway* sort of life. She could get on with her life and have a fresh future despite any past mistakes or bad choices. John 4:39 reported that this woman had new life as an evangelist for Jesus. Many Samaritans from that city believed in him because of the woman's testimony.

Later in John 11, Jesus raised his friend Lazarus up to this new life or *zway*. Jesus as the giver of new life is one recurring theme in John's gospel. The young man in the opening illustration had to deal with bitter legal and embittered ex-spouse opposition. Jesus dealt with opposition which led to his death after he healed Lazarus. Jesus stayed on mission. His hour (John 2) had not arrived yet. In our lesson today, the bread and wine symbolize and represent the new life Jesus provided when his hour of crucifixion would arrive John 3:16; John 18-19 (RSV). His death would not be the final word, there was new life indeed.

On this day, Jesus announced he was the Bread of Life. He invited listeners into a relationship with him. The body and blood of his sacrifice was to be the final Passover or deliverance act as experienced in the meal of bread and wine. This is a metaphor for Jesus' own sacrifice for the sins of humanity as is summarized in John 3:16. Following Jesus as Messiah is not merely listening to teachings and intellectually assenting to what Jesus says. It is partaking and being active in living out visible symbols such as a bread and wine.

John 6 is an example of Jesus putting his best effort into the ministry the Father sent him to carry on in our midst. Jesus is actually God in the flesh John 1:14 (RSV). He had fed five thousand people. He had taught them. In this text, he reminded the listeners that partaking in this meal of Thanksgiving (Eucharist) points to the body and blood he was giving for the sins of humanity. Rather than gratitude for his ministry, it is stated in John 6:66 "After this many of his disciples drew back and no longer went about with him." Later, Jesus said to the twelve, "Do you also wish to go away?" Simon Peter answered him, "Lord, to whom shall we go? You have the words of eternal life" John 6:67-68 (RSV). John is unique here among the other gospels.

Rather than selecting the twelve disciples at another time such as a fishing event or at the tax collector's booth, the final twelve disciples are the ones who stayed with Jesus despite what other disciples considered unacceptable sayings or teachings. They were the ones who did not walk away or reject Jesus. Also, in John, Simon Peter asked, "Lord to whom shall we go?" The disciples acknowledged and followed Jesus as Lord. In the season of Pentecost, the good news is that Jesus remains our Lord in rejection, like the young man in the opening illustration who was experiencing divorce.

Because Jesus experienced rejection from people whom he thought were his disciples, he knows how we feel about the same sort of rejection. Jesus knows how a person who is no longer on the sports team, cheerleading squad, or working for the major employer in the community feels when their best efforts are rejected, and are left alone without the people they thought to be their friends. The words of Jesus remain intact, "…he who eats my flesh and drinks my blood has eternal life, and I will raise him up at the last day. For my flesh is food indeed, and my blood is drink indeed. He who eats my flesh and drinks my blood abides in me, and I in him. As the living Father sent me, and I live because of the Father, so he who eats me will live because of me" John 6:54-56 (RSV).

If Jesus is our Lord, life goes on. It is a vibrant, forward moving new adventure that continues. We get to turn the page in the book of life despite any past rejections. And yes, we can put our best foot forward and still be rejected. If Jesus is our Lord, this need not be the last final word in our lives. We will have life and have it abundantly John 10:10 (RSV). This is the good news of the gospel today.

The young man and father in the opening illustration did indeed weather many messy divorce court hearings. He learned that lawyers were not such bad people despite how the popular media portrayed them. There were people whom he thought to be friends, who kept their distance from him as if he were a modern day leper. Also, there were people with whom he could share his deepest feelings and hurtful experiences who proved to be true, sincere friends and companions during that painful journey of divorce. He did go on to get advanced degrees and certifications in his vocation. He did indeed move up the success ladder in his field. He was able to retire early. He also found another mate who had also experienced a divorce with her children. They now have a blended family. It is new life for this family indeed. The new middle-aged man's skills and abilities in his vocation remained valid despite any unfortunate past messy marital problems. His daughter eventually went onto the university, got a job and is married with a child. Life does go on! When our best efforts are rejected, we can take a page out of the playbook of Simon Peter and ask, "Lord, to whom shall we go? You have the words of eternal life;" These words are our new life on this Sunday in Pentecost. We can now to get on with our new, forward moving lives as Christians and a congregation on this Sunday in Pentecost.

Amen.

Sources:

Johannes Beutler, S.J., *A Commentary on the Gospel of John,* (Grand Rapids, MI: Wm. B. Erdmann's, 2017).

Andrew T. Lincoln, *Black's New Testament Commentary: The Gospel According to John,* (Peabody, MA: Hendrickson Publishers, 2005).

J. Louis Martyn, *History & Theology in the Fourth Gospel,* (Nashville, TN: Abingdon Press, 1968).

Barclay Newman, *Greek-English Dictionary of the New Testament,* (London, UK: United Bible Societies, 1971).

When The Rules Change

A couple who lived in separate apartments fell in love and decided to get married. However, both of their parents informed them that they would have to finance their own wedding, reception and honeymoon. In the good old days in that community, it was one of the couples' parents who carried much of the financial burden for weddings. The couple decided it was prudent to live together in one apartment, and use the money saved for their wedding plans. For the more traditional people in their church, this is called "shacking up" and "immoral behavior." The couple believed the rules had changed when it came to who pays for the weddings in their family and community.

In the same community, a young person recently graduated from the state university. They worked during the summers and obtained as much financial aid as possible. After graduation, they were confronted with an enormous student loan payment plan. Their new job in the college major they studied did not pay well for newer employees. The adult college graduate returned home and was living in her parents' house. The parents, from a different generation held to the belief that they had raised their young person and they went off to college. Their adult child was now living back home for the foreseeable future. Again, the rules have changed.

A university-educated state employee had been in his position for over twenty years. He thought that his retirement pension program was secure and could continue working for the state for another ten years. The bombshell announcement occurred when the state was in financial trouble. All state employee pension programs were under water. The state would no longer be able to honor the commitments made to their employees. Furthermore, the state was doing drastic human resources reductions. The workers with the most amount of seniority had been asked to depart from their position with a very small cash payment. This employee was in his late fifties of age, and faced a very competitive employment market with younger candidates. The employee watched the television to relieve stress, only to see commercials on how to earn a college degree for success. The rules had changed on this worker. He had practiced a strong Christian work ethic all of his life and now wondered if he would ever be able to retire. As the saying goes, "All of the people tried to live by the rules, with the assumption the rules will keep them." Now the rules had changed!

Using terms from the Mediterranean New Testament times, these people have been ejected from the "in group" to the "out group" of their times. For example, at one time, having a higher level education implied one was within the mainstream of the growing middle class in North America. Now one must have the right college major and entry into the right field at the best time for income and opportunity. The engaged couple who desired to get married were also not part of the in-group because their extended family was no longer supporting their wedding in monetary manner. The rules had changed on these people.

During the New Testament days, it was quite fluid as to who was part of the in-group and out group as well. The fortunes of one's family and extended family could change with a bad crop or foreign country invasion. Quite often, this made people instant outsiders of their time as such as the people who lost their jobs and less than supportive extended families. As one watches the news, in the foreseeable future, artificial intelligence may displace more people in their jobs, education opportunities, and may challenge the power arrangements that many people in leadership roles have relied upon.

In Jesus' times, the temple leaders created their own interpretation of the Jewish Torah Laws on food into a stringent dogma or doctrine for average working citizens. Such leaders strictly enforced boundaries in order to keep themselves in power so they can continually to be part of the "in-group" who enjoyed the privileges that out group people did not experience (Malina, 373).

Immediately after this reading, Jesus healed a Gentile or non-Jewish Syrophoenician woman's daughter, and later a deaf man in the region of Tyre, north of Galilee. Jesus was the Messiah who addressed people who had experienced the rules changing in ways that altered their lives in major ways. As national leaders in Rome either died or got assassinated, inevitable the rules changed again (Malina, 397-398).

How can we live as faithful Christians in times when the rules change on us? Mark's gospel lays out three strands of Jesus' ministry which could be applied to our discipleship journey today. First, in Mark, Jesus did everything "immediately." The Greek word *euthos* is used 42 times in Mark's gospel. This makes Mark the shortest of the four gospels.

In today's terms, Jesus had a list of tasks or duties to do, and he moved on from task to task. Even while being tempted by Satan in the wilderness; it took all of two verses in Mark 1:14-15. There is no dialogue with Satan about turning stones into bread or jumping off the temple as in Matthew and Luke. We do not get a Sermon on the Mount in Mark as in Matthew. Nor do we hear parables about the prodigal son or good Samaritan as in Luke. Jesus was like the worker who kept his nose to the grindstone and kept working. He might be the unemployed person who was always on the computer at employment websites and sending resumes to prospective employers. He was like the couple who had a "to do" list in planning their wedding, and aggressively attacked the list with check marks by each item. This is one tool for discipleship that Jesus in Mark offers us today — we should do tasks immediately. Do not procrastinate!

Second, Jesus did have many tasks going on at the same time. In Mark 5, while Jesus is *en route* to healing Jairus' daughter, he also healed a hemorrhaging woman and made sure she knew that it was her faith that also helped in her healing. Jesus was the modern person who might have an art or wood project going in the back room or in the shed, while they were working on cooking a meal for the family — with the cell phone on, awaiting calls from friends who serve as "network" partners to find another position or business opportunity.

In Mark's gospel, Jesus' mission is stated in Mark 10:45, "For the son of man also came not to be served but to serve, and to give his life as a ransom for many." The reason Jesus wanted people to keep silent regarding his healing, exorcising demons, and transfiguration meeting with Moses and Elijah, is that the true nature of being a "Messiah" is "to give his life as a ransom for many" on the cross Mark 15 (RSV). What is a person willing to sacrifice for a higher cause or goal in life? This is one challenge Mark's gospel presents to us as a church in this Pentecost season.

In the process of doing all tasks immediately and having many projects going on at the same time, Jesus realized that the disciples may or may not "catch on" to what he was all about as "Messiah." In Mark, Jesus was the suffering servant tradition of Isaiah 52-53. He had to be prepared for one or more of this disciples to jump ship when the going got tough Mark 14:50 (RSV). Therefore, he had to train and teach as many disciples as possible. By today's standards, his teaching would have not only been in book form, but on a blog or CD and he would have left both a paper trail and cyber cloud media set of messages. For modern job seekers and the couple who are seeking to get married as soon as possible, this means thinking outside the box. Also, as this relates to Mark 7, one must ask what is the result or outcome of the particular purity, politically correct or implied traditions of the day? When the rules change, such laws either may nor may not be helpful. Would the Christian couple be willing to use the WICCA temple fellowship hall for their reception, if they were offered a reasonable cost arrangement?

Another example might be a resume section with community activities that show organizational and people skills that may be more beneficial in the job market than another academic degree. The couple in the opening illustration might also take in a paying boarder to help with the financial burdens of raising money for a wedding. The unemployed state employee might want to seek a position as a lobbyist for one of the private sector companies who seeks to have their views heard in the government sector. By some standards, these might be considered less than "ethical" actions. However, when the rules changed, Jesus had to revisit the reasons why certain food laws were in place in our lesson.

Finally, after the empty tomb event, the young man in the white robe told the women, "But go, tell his disciples and Peter that he is going before you to Galilee; there you will see him, as he told you" Mark 16:7 (RSV). Galilee was the less domesticated area of Judea where more bandits and unsettled peoples wandered. It was further from the city of Jerusalem. It was the place where the cell phone signals dropped, there was slow internet service and where illegal immigrants might sneak into without being caught by the authorities. The bottom line here was that Jesus told his disciples not to geographically restrict themselves in terms of the next place to do ministry and carry out one's life's mission.

When the rules change in the city, one's own school alma mater might have too many "hanging-on" alumni seeking jobs. The traditional employers may be in the driver's seat when it comes to being selective among a larger pool of candidates in tight, competitive, employment market. One example might be the same music teacher whose application is in a sea of fifty or more applicants in the urban area where they attended the university, might be one of only four applicants in a remote rural state which does not have many of the pay perks as in the Jerusalem or urban locations. Jesus told his disciples who had abandoned him on the cross that he was willing to still work with them, despite their shortcomings. However, he would meet them in Galilee. Where is the Galilee for people today who seek opportunities? He works with us today in our church here despite our mistakes and shortcomings. Many of us are simply in a world where the rules have changed on us. We kept the rules, but the rules did not keep us.

Finally, because Jesus died on the cross for the sins of humanity and rose from the grave three days later, there are many second chances. Christianity is a religion of second chances. Mark 16:8 ends abruptly. It is like watching a television series and suddenly, the programming credits cut in during the climatic action scenes. The ending is unknown. The viewer is left to write their own ending. This is also the good news in Mark's gospel. We get to write the ending of our own lives - regardless of past mistakes. The rules have changed and yes, we may feel like we are being abandoned by those who we thought were our friends. We get to write the final chapter of our own life journey in Mark's gospel. This is how Mark presents the good news while realizing the rules change in life and he is keeping it real.

Amen.

Source:

John R. Donahue, S.J., and Daniel J. Harrington, *Sacra Pagina: The Gospel of Mark,* (Collegeville, MN: The Liturgical Press, 2002).

Bruce J. Malina, and Richard Rohrbaugh, *Social Science Commentary: On the Synoptic Gospels,* (Minneapolis, MN: Augsburg Fortress, 2003) 373.

Katharine Doob, Sakenfeld, Editor, *The New Interpreter's Dictionary of the Bible, Volume 2,* (Nashville, TN: Abingdon Press, 2007).

www.ingramcontent.com/pod-product-compliance
Lightning Source LLC
LaVergne TN
LVHW091208080426
835509LV00006B/893